The Evaluation
of
Social Policies

INTERNATIONAL SERIES IN SOCIAL WELFARE

Series Editor:

William J. Reid
State University of New York at Albany

The Evaluation
of
Social Policies

JOHN A. CRANE

KLUWER·NIJHOFF PUBLISHING
BOSTON/THE HAGUE/LONDON

DISTRIBUTORS FOR NORTH AMERICA:
Kluwer Boston, Inc.
190 Old Derby Street
Hingham, Massachusetts 02043, U.S.A.

DISTRIBUTORS OUTSIDE NORTH AMERICA:
Kluwer Academic Publishers Group
Distribution Centre
P.O. Box 322
3300 AH Dordrecht, The Netherlands

Library of Congress Cataloging in Publication Data

Crane, John A.
  The evaluation of social policies.

  (International series in social welfare)
  Bibliography: p.
  Includes index.
  1. Social service—Research. 2. Evaluation
research (Social action programs) 3. Social
policy—Evaluation. I. Title. II. Series.
HV11.C792   361.6′1′072   81–20828
ISBN 0–89838–075–8   AACR2

To Evariste Thériault for his active interest; special thanks to Dennis Kimberley for his detailed critique.

To the National Welfare Grants Division of Health and Welfare Canada for their financial support.

To Irene and Alan, for their psychological support; to Roy Francis, who started all this; to Richard Berk, Sidney Duder, Forrest Hansen, Camille Lambert, George Maslany, Sheila Neysmith, and Daniel O'Brien for helpful comments on earlier formulations.

To Carolyn Hudnall and Robert Wang for excellent research assistance; to James Kalbfleisch, D. A. Sprott, and James Zidek for consultation and guidance.

To the Canadian Association of Schools of Social Work for providing the project with a much needed home base and effective administration.

CONTENTS

Introduction   1
Policy Evaluation and Evaluation Policy   1
Evaluation as a Discipline   2
Purposes of This Study   3
Treatment of Methods   4
Plan   5
Level of Difficulty of Presentation   5

I VALUATION

1 Issues in Evaluation Policy   9
An Overview of Evaluation Approaches   9
A Schema for Comparing Approaches   12

2 Evaluation and Social Research   19
Evaluation as Scientific Theory Testing   19
Limitations of the Scientific Theory-Testing Approach   23
Evaluation as Applied Scientific Methods   24
The Applied Scientific Methods Approach: A Critique   28
The Problem of Naturalism in Evaluation   29
Evaluation as Directed Social Change   32
Limitations of Evaluation as Directed Social Change   38

3 Evaluation and Social Justice   40
A Utilitarian Perspective on Policy Evaluation   40
An Egalitarian Perspective   43
The Egalitarian Perspective on Nuclear Power   46

Inequality in the Social Services 50
The Egalitarian Approach: A Critique 52

4 A Framework for Valuation 53
Evaluation as a Form of Social Inquiry 53
Context and Scope of Valuation 54
Relating Valuations to Observations 58
Comprehensive Evaluation 61
Appropriate Policies to Guide Uncertain Inferences 65
Roles of Scientist and Citizen in Valuation 67

II VALUATION AND OBSERVATION

5 Technique of Value Scaling 73
The Outcome Measure and the Value Scale 74
Magnitude Estimation 76
Method of Obtaining Magnitude Estimates: Exhibit 1 78
Finding Relative Origins: Exhibit 2 80
Meaning of the Relative Origin 81
Understanding Power Functions of Outcome Scores 81
Bipolar Value Scales 82
Multiple Measures of Effect for Each Value Scale 82
Units of the Value Scale 83
Magnitude Estimation and Social Dissension 83
Magnitude Estimation as a Tool of Social Evaluation 84

6 Relationships That Determine Outcomes of Tests of Hypotheses 86
The Outcome Probability 86
Formulating the Null and Threshold Hypotheses 87
The Discrepancy Measure (D) as a Proxy for the Outcome Probability 88
Direct Determinants of the Outcome Probability 89
Unreliability, Invalidity, and Sample Variances 90
Effects of Inconsistent Intervention Effects 91
Effects of Protection against Type 1 and Type 2 Errors on Sample Size Requirements 93
Recapitulation 96

7 Squaring Research Design with Policy Requirements 97
Specification of Values: An Example 97
Measurement Design 98

Outcome Measure   98
Magnitude Estimation of Effectiveness   99
Patterning of Observations   100
Formulating the Threshold Hypothesis   100
Determining an Optimum Level of Protection against
   Type 1 and Type 2 Errors   100
Variations in the Research Design by Types of
   Evaluation Questions   105
Recapitulation   107
The Problem of Generalizing from Policy Evaluation   108

III   OBSERVATION AND INFERENCE

8   Plausible and Implausible Hypotheses   113
Specification of Hypotheses   113
The Measurement of Plausibility   114
Likelihood Inference   115
Maximum Likelihood   115
Likelihood Functions   118
Relative Likelihood   119
Joint Relative Likelihood Analysis: An Example   121

9   Fluctuating Parameters   125
Local Probabilistic Systems   126
Diachronic Sampling   126
Bayesian Inference   127
Sources of the Prior Distribution   129
Forms and Uses of Posterior Distribution   131
Bayesian Decision Rules   131

10   A Classification of Evaluative Inference Methods   137
Overview of the Classification   137
No Prior Data; Dichotomous Value Scale: Case 1   140
Prior Information; Dichotomous Value Scale: Case 2   142
No Prior Data; Ratio Value Scale: Case 3   143
Prior Information; Ratio Value Scale: Case 4   144

IV   TWO CASE STUDIES IN EVALUATION

11   Technical Skew in Social Work Evaluations   149
Essentials of TECH   149
The Prevalence of TECH   151

Two Examples of TECH in Social Work Research   151
Planned and Unplanned Features of TECH-Mode
    Designs   152
Implicit Threshold Hypotheses   154
Taking Account of Type 1 and Type 2 Errors   157

**12 A Reanalysis of Love Canal Data on Spontaneous
     Abortions**   161
The Scientific Controversies   161
The Question of Controls in the Studies of
    Birth Abnormalities   163
Plan of Reanalysis of the Data on Miscarriages   164
Relative Likelihood Analysis   167
Implications   169

**Appendix: Evaluating Likelihoods Using an Electronic
Calculator or the Computer**   171
Calculating Joint Relative Likelihoods for Binomial
    Populations Using an Electronic Calculator   172
Program: Binomial Likelihoods   175
Program: "Example Run"   181
Extension to the Multinomial Case: Calculation of
    Multinomial Likelihoods Using a Desk or Hand
    Calculator   183
Program S.Multi   186
Calculating Relative Likelihoods for a Poisson Mean
    Using an Electronic Calculator   191
Program Poisson   193
Program Poisson: A Sample Run   196
Calculation of the Maximum Relative Likelihood for
    the Mean of a Normal Sample Using an Electronic
    Calculator   198
Program Normal Likelihoods   200
Notes   203

References   205

Name Index   213

Subject Index   217

The Evaluation
of
Social Policies

INTRODUCTION

POLICY EVALUATION AND EVALUATION POLICY

The term *policy evaluation* is used in this study to mean the appraisal of policies in the light of data collected by standardized research procedures. The appraisal is guided by one or more of the following values: inclusiveness of coverage, adequacy, equitableness, appropriate citizen involvement, and effectiveness. Elaborations of these terms and justification for selecting them are developed in the first part of the study.

Other terms employed include the following:

Policy: a commitment to a course of action based on broad plans and general principles. Examples include setting an acceptable level of exposure to vinyl chloride airborne particles in a factory or, perhaps, use of family casework to reduce the number of children entering foster care.

Policy formulation: (1) the substance of policy as expressed in legislation, agreements or directives; or (2) the process of arriving at a particular policy.

Policy implementation: standing arrangements (programs) for putting policy into effect.

1

Policy outcomes: planned and unplanned consequences of policy implementation.

Scope of evaluation: includes policy formulation (process or product), implementation, or outcomes.

Evaluation variables: characteristics of the policy on which data are to be collected for the purpose of evaluation. Combining the three possible concerns of evaluation with the five values mentioned above yields fifteen classes of evaluation variables.

Policy areas: (1) the social services (e.g., social work, education, income maintenance, workers' compensation, and health); and (2) control of hazardous technologies. The rationale for bringing these two main policy areas together is given below.

Evaluation policies: policy decisions made by evaluators of social policies. These involve the selection of values to be applied, definition of significant findings, decisions as to the roles to be played in the evaluation by scientists and citizens, and selection of policies to guide uncertain inferences. Finally, evaluators must select optimum methods of observation, measurement, and data analysis.

EVALUATION AS A DISCIPLINE

In recent years there has been a growing recognition of common problems in evaluation in the many different fields in which it is conducted. Arguably, evaluation has already emerged as a distinctive discipline (Glass, 1976; Anderson and Ball, 1978; Cronbach and Associates, 1980). One proof of this would be agreement on an agenda of problems basic to evaluation per se and not reducible to problems of economics, statistics, or any other field. By this test, the discipline of evaluation hardly seems to have arrived. There is no well-established consensus on how the problems of evaluation policy and method referred to above should be formulated. These problems lie unspoken beneath many debates over the interpretation of findings. Chapter 1 contains a sampling of recent debates that illustrate this point.

Clarification of issues is rendered more difficult by the continued sharp division of the evaluation enterprise into a concern with social service policies on the one hand and policies designed to protect the public interest (for example, from the hazardous technologies) on the other. Though the same problems of evaluation policy and method arise in each of these areas, they continue to be dealt with in separate realms, each staffed by its own cadre of professionals who have produced two largely unrelated bodies of literature. Thus the recent works by Rowe (1976), Shrader-Frechette (1980), and Collingridge (1980) on risk and control of threatening technologies make use of references hardly mentioned in the works on social program evaluation by Attkisson and Others (1978), Rossi, Freeman, and Wright (1979), and Cronbach and Associates (1980).

Not only are the problems of evaluation policy and method in these two areas very similar, but the social problems with which they are concerned are interacting. As traditionally described (e.g., by Cronbach and Associates, 1980, p. 107), evaluation research begins with the identification of a social problem and proceeds to the assessment of alternative efforts to deal with the problem. But one group's social problem is often a result of another group's social program. Many of the homeless men in a western Canadian city, for example, are disabled former employees of the forest industries, victims of hazardous working conditions — an unintended result of policies designed to increase productivity and to improve Canada's export trade. An increasing proportion of total resources for health and welfare will be expended in coming decades on victims of these and other occupational hazards (Weiler, 1980, p. 137). Similarly, an increase in the incidence of radiation-induced health problems in the general population will be one outcome of policies supporting a reliance on nuclear power (Shrader-Frechette, 1980, p. 43).

Thus the need for and adequacy of social services are increasingly a function of policy decisions about hazards. The need for a common evaluative framework in these two realms is illustrated by the contradictory recommendations on the control of lead emissions by automobiles made by two groups of English policy analysts. One group, concerned with deregulation of the automobile industry, recommended that as sound industrial strategy, no reduction in emissions be required; the other group, concerned with children's health problems, recommended a reduction in emissions based on evidence that exposure to lead is a cause of mental retardation (*Manchester Guardian*, 1981).

PURPOSES OF THIS STUDY

The purposes of this study are to spell out in more detail current issues in evaluation policy; to examine critically the contemporary approaches to these issues; and to offer the basics of an alternative approach, including those methods needed to apply it which are not readily accessible to evaluators.

In broad outline, the issues in evaluation policy addressed in this study are:

Valuation: selection of values to be applied; admissible and inadmissible values; contexts of valuation; sources of values; the problem of conflicts among values.

Valuation and observation: the role of values in instrument creation; value scaling; definition of policy-significant findings.

Scientists' and citizens' roles: evaluation as a form of inquiry involving both the sciences and the humanities; the problem of distinguishing technical decisions from policy judgments; selection and use of members of client groups or of populations at risk as judges in constructing value scales; validity and fairness of valuation procedures.

Policies to govern uncertain inferences: the relationship of valuation, observation and inference; conventional versus specially designed inference policies; single-school versus eclectic approaches to inference.

In terms of these policy issues, evaluation may be defined as follows: *evaluation = valuation + observation + inference*.

TREATMENT OF METHODS

As a result of the enhanced opportunities during the 1960s and 1970s to put evaluation methods to use on a large scale, methods developed rapidly and many textbooks appeared (e.g., Scioli and Cook, 1975; Bennett and Lumsdaine, 1975; Fairweather and Tornatzky, 1977; Jöreskog and Sörbom, 1979; Rossi, Freeman, and Wright, 1979). Probably no single work can do justice to the array of sophisticated methods now available.

This study concentrates on methodological problems encountered in applying the framework developed in the early chapters. The following topics are stressed:

Transformation of descriptive measures into value scales.

Use of ratio scaling coupled with curve fitting to identify the "threshold" point on the value scale — that is, the point at which a finding becomes significant from a policy perspective; with no implication of causality, the term *threshold effect* is occasionally employed for this value.

Use of panels of citizen-raters for value scaling and to make judgments concerning type 1 and type 2 errors. (A type 1 error consists of falsely concluding that a policy has some specified characteristic; a type 2 error consists of falsely concluding the opposite.)

Working out the quantitative relationships between threshold effects and research design factors (sample size, variance, measurement error, treatment consistency, type 1 and type 2 error levels) to clarify design requirements.

Setting research design factors to conform fully to the value and policy requirements initially established.

Measurement of the relative plausibility of competing hypotheses. Concepts taken from the likelihood inference school of statistics (Edwards, 1972) are used for this purpose. In view of the inaccessibility of this material to most evaluators, it is treated in detail; worked out examples and computer programs are appended.

Taking account of fluctuations in policy variables. For this purpose, Bayesian concepts and examples are employed. In view of the recent appearance of a large nontechnical literature on Bayesian statistics, only an introduction to the Bayesian system is included in this study; applications to evaluation problems are emphasized.

Classification of inference methods to suit the available types of value scales, degree of instability of policy variables, and availability of prior information. Using these factors, a typology of ten algorithms of inference suitable for policy evaluation studies is developed.

PLAN

In Part I, Valuation, seven representative current approaches are appraised with respect to a scheme of critical issues. Based on these reviews, an alternative approach to these issues is proposed.

Part II picks up on a key issue: relating valuations to observations. Chapter 5 considers values and data and proposes a method of identifying significant findings. Once the important data points are identified, they are used to frame hypotheses, which in turn shape the research design (Chapters 6 and 7). Part III moves on to problems of inference and generalization in Chapters 8, 9, and 10. The emphasis is on probabilistic inference, although nonprobabilistic inference is also considered. The last two chapters (11 and 12) are case studies in evaluation in the social services and in research on the risk of birth abnormalities associated with exposure to toxic industrial wastes. Using the framework developed in the first part, the data are reanalyzed, and a different perspective on the findings is offered.

LEVEL OF DIFFICULTY OF PRESENTATION

Technical topics are treated at an elementary level. Adequate background for making use of this work is an introductory course in social research methods and statistical inference. Occasional cross-reference is made to a book by Spiegel (1961), *Statistics*, in the Schaum's Outline Series.

I VALUATION

1 ISSUES IN EVALUATION POLICY

AN OVERVIEW OF EVALUATION APPROACHES

The term *paradigm*, referring to the set of all forms containing important elements in common, is useful in gaining an overview of contemporary approaches to policy evaluation. These approaches derive from three paradigms of inquiry: scientific research, directed social change, and theory of social justice. Table 1.1 classifies seven approaches by the paradigms of inquiry of which they are members.

Table 1.1. Paradigms of Inquiry and Approaches to Policy Evaluation

Paradigm	Approach
Scientific research	Scientific theory testing
	Applied scientific research methods
Directed social change	Utilization-focused evaluation
	Evaluation as education
	Qualitative case study
Theory of social justice	Egalitarian evaluation
	Utilitarian evaluation

These seven approaches are hardly unique in all respects. The proponents of evaluation as education, for example, advocate the use of scientific methods whenever possible. Utilitarian values can be found beneath the surface of many scientific evaluations. In fact, utilitarianism and egalitarianism share a number of assumptions. Notwithstanding these similarities, the seven approaches differ in what they regard as central and peripheral to policy evaluation. Each approach leads to a distinctive point of view on the issues of evaluation policy listed in the Introduction.

Scientific Research

In one approach, scientific theory testing, a model predicting the effects of policies is adopted from some field of social or natural science. This model is chosen because the predicted outcomes are considered important to policy making; if the policy is concerned, for example, with the problem of drug addiction, the model may specify the factors that affect addictive behavior. These factors must be manipulable. The theory provides a test of the policy, and the evaluation, in turn, becomes a test of the theory.

The areas of social science that have most often been applied in this way are economics and learning theory. Economic theories have supplied a model for income maintenance experiments (Tuma and Robins, 1980) and for many evaluations of correctional programs. Learning theory has served to guide many experiments in education. The work of Hamblin et al. (1971) illustrates these applications. Policy evaluations in areas such as the effects of low-level radiation on human populations may make use of models from the biological sciences, physics, or epidemiology. A current illustration is a paper on the interpretation of Hiroshima and Nagasaki data on the health effects of low-level radiation (Rotblat, 1981).

Most policy and program evaluation today borrows the methods but not the theories of science. The evaluator is assumed to be a technologist rather than a science theorist. Competence in evaluation is the ability to apply appropriate research methods to problems whose content is determined by policy and planning considerations. Methods are assumed to have a logic of their own, uniquely suited to the problem of assessing the net effects of policies.

A major source of inspiration for this approach has been work on the design of experiments, especially in psychology and social psychology (Campbell and Stanley, 1963). A collection of research methodologies designed in part to approximate experiments has also been developed. Three recent textbooks in which this approach to evaluation is set forth are by

Scioli and Cook (1975), Attkisson and Others (1978), and Rossi, Freeman, and Wright (1979).

Directed Social Change

The participants in evaluation are almost invariably changed by the experience — an argument by some that this is the real point of the exercise. To be useful, evaluation findings must be acted on. Coming to grips with the problem of formulating evaluation questions is a journey of discovery. At each step, different partisans argue for different courses of action; each decision must be negotiated. The special skill of the evaluator lies in guiding or facilitating the process of discovery and change. Science and methodology are part of this process but hardly serve to define it. Competence in evaluation is defined, rather, as the ability to provide social change consultation based on research data.

This approach dates back to the work of Kurt Lewin and followers in the 1940s. Three contemporary versions are utilization-focused evaluation (Patton, 1978), evaluation as education (Cronbach and Associates, 1980), and the qualitative case study (Stake, 1978).

Social Justice

Evaluation can be viewed as neither science nor technology but as applied social philosophy. One version of this has its roots in egalitarian theories of social justice, especially the theory of John Rawls, who asserted that the conception of justice provides a standard for assessing the distributive aspects of a social system (Rawls, 1972, p. 9). A deeper root of this approach is Kantian theory of morality (Fried, 1970; Donagan, 1977).

Perhaps the most important difference of the egalitarian approach from the foregoing five approaches is in the evaluator's prior commitment to policy missions. Proponents of the scientific, methodological, and social change models take the mission of a particular set of policy makers as given; evaluators who question the aims of the mission should find other projects with which they are in greater sympathy (Cronbach and Associates, 1980, p. 211).

The egalitarians, on the other hand, attempt a much more searching analysis of the aims and effects of policies and missions. Instead of accepting a given set of policies as a context for their work, they try to create a context and agenda for social policy making. Their work is not to be limited to fine tuning of policies assumed to be essentially sound; nor do they see themselves as condemned to be professional meliorists, as do the advocates of evaluation as education (Cronbach and Associates, 1980, p. 157).

This observation applies also to *utilitarianism*, the philosophical underpinning for a rapidly growing and influential body of criticism of the policies of the welfare state. This approach is illustrated by a recent collection of studies on domestic and foreign policies in the United States (Duignan and Rabushka, 1980). The utilitarian perspective is of interest not only in its own right, but also because it provides insights into often unrecognized value assumptions underlying the scientific, methodological, and change consultation approaches. Moreover, by furnishing a contrasting critique of social policies, the utilitarian perspective helps to illuminate the egalitarian perspective.

A SCHEMA FOR COMPARING APPROACHES

The schema presented here is an elaboration of the policy evaluation issues listed in the Introduction, and it serves to guide the comparative analysis of the seven approaches discussed in Chapters 2 and 3.

Valuation

Admissible and Inadmissible Values; Exclusive and Inclusive Policies.   Valuation entails making value judgments concerning policy formulation, implementation, or outcomes. Evaluators, however, differ strongly as to the values that may appropriately be applied. Some, for example, insist that only such trite values as cost or efficiency, on which there is no problem arriving at a consensus, may legitimately be included (Collingridge, 1981, pp. 161–71); vague concepts such as equity must be relegated to the realm of politics. Other evaluators (e.g., Shrader-Frechette, 1980) argue for an inclusive policy. They have no scientific qualms about including all values they find relevant. The former view is characteristic of evaluators who adopt a scientific approach, and the latter view is characteristic of the egalitarians. Debates over public policy on nuclear power, workers' compensation, and income maintenance illustrate this difference.

   1.   *Nuclear power.* A paper by a member of the U.S. Nuclear Regulatory Commission, the body charged with evaluating public policy on nuclear power, dismisses ethical, social, and political variables as being ex-

traneous and irrelevant, serving only to cloud debate (Doub, 1974, p. 262). In contrast, a recent study of this area of public policy has found the research on which policy has been based to be narrowly technical, focused on economic and utilitarian concerns to the exclusion of human rights, and oblivious to the ethical and political dimensions of allegedly technical issues (Shrader-Frechette, 1980, p. 157).

2. *Efficiency versus equity in workers' compensation.* Workers' compensation is commonly viewed as a substitute for a free market exchange between workers and employers. In the free market workers seek redress for injuries through the courts. Since this system fails to work effectively in practice, workers have given up the right to sue in exchange for a more secure and predictable scale of compensation. To evaluate this program, one inquires into its possible disruptive effects on the market economy. In particular, program costs must be kept low enough so that the competitive position of industry will not be undermined — an especially important point for economies that are dependent on foreign trade.

This view of evaluation dovetails nicely with the scientific paradigm of evaluation. Aiming for objective, replicable findings, research attempts to reduce value judgments to factual questions. One way is to conflate all measures into monetary units; another is to concentrate on those aspects of policy that can be studied scientifically.

In line with these views of the program and of research, two major studies of workers' compensation in British Columbia, undertaken in 1975, focused on problems of minimizing costs and maximizing management effectiveness (Eckler and Segal & Co. Ltd., 1975; Ross and Partners, 1976). One of the studies defined its problem as actuarial science and the other as management science.

A recent policy paper challenges these perceptions of workers' compensation and of evaluation research and argues that this program should be understood not as an economic measure but as a social welfare policy — one of a set of policies aimed at protection against the financial effects of disablement (Ison, 1977). The program should be evaluated against standards of adequacy and equity — that is, responsiveness to all kinds of work-induced disablements and the fairness of benefits. As presently constituted, workers' compensation responds effectively to injuries at work but not to work-induced illness. Persons disabled from causes that are not work related receive far less adequate benefits.

To meet Ison's proposed objectives, evaluation could not restrict itself to value-free descriptive measurement, nor to problems to which scientific methods are readily applicable. "Fairness," "adequacy," and "equity" cannot be reduced to monetary scales nor to questions of fact. Evaluation must in this view devise ways of mapping observations over a wider range of values than just cost or monetary benefits.

3. *Income maintenance.* During the 1970s, some $325 million were spent in the United States on income maintenance experiments designed to measure the effects of guaranteed annual income plans on the incentive to work (Aaron, 1978, p. 174). Economic theories served to structure the experiments, which then served as a test of the theories. Recently a noted policy analyst attacked the experimental plan as being limited, incomplete, and misleading to the public (Goodwin, 1979). The critic argued that the outcome measures were concentrated too heavily on economic variables and provided inadequate data on the effects of the experiment on family behavior. In reply, the researchers pointed out that they were primarily engaged in testing an economic theory, that they could not offer value judgments about family life, and that they sought only to create a factual basis for policy making (Hannan et al., 1979).

Contexts of Valuation. Valuations are made in personal, standard, or ideal contexts (Kaplan, 1964, p. 390). The first are purely personal preferences, the second are ascriptions of what x sample of persons would find to be valuable under specified circumstances, and the third are judgments of what is best for society or humankind in the long run. Approaches to evaluation differ in the degree to which these different contexts of valuation are recognized and taken into account. Often, only personal contexts — those of the evaluators themselves — are considered.

Sources of Values. Science is the principal, if not the sole, source of values for many evaluators. Others look to the wants of decision makers and consumers of services, and still others appeal to theories of justice and morality.

Conflicts and Trade-offs among Values. An inclusive policy toward values raises a number of problems. The first is how one can defend a particular set of values as complete and appropriate to the problem at hand. Since values may collide (for example, efficiency may be purchased at the cost of equity), priority rules and principles by which the rules can be justified are needed.

Conflicting assumptions about the appropriate contexts of valuation and values that should govern the evaluation process itself are illustrated by current debates between the proponents of evaluation as scientific inquiry and those who see it as directed social change. In a recent text on evaluation, the position is taken that systematic, as opposed to casual, evaluation is defined by the use of scientific methods of gathering valid and reliable evidence (Rossi, Freeman, and Wright, 1979, p. 31).

This position has been sharply attacked by a second group of evaluation researchers who urge evaluators to move away from the model of evaluation as scientific research methodology (Cronbach and Associates, 1980, p. 55). In part, this view is based on skepticism about claims to rigorous assessment, but the major argument is that outcomes carry very little weight in policy making and are therefore relatively unimportant. As a mere producer of information, the evaluator is a voice in the wilderness. Evaluation findings should be judged not by their scientific rigor but by their "leverage." To have real impact, evaluations must be planned and carried out in close conjunction with policy making. The overriding value for evaluation is usefulness to the policy-making community.

Relating Values to Observations: The Valuation Process

Values and Instrumentation. Once a set of values has been chosen, problems arise as to the role these values should play in data collection and measurement. One problem is whether and how to use values to guide the construction of data collection schedules.

Value Scales. After the data are collected, a decision must be made as to the need for a formal process of mapping the original observations onto a value scale. Alternatively, this transformation can be carried out informally by judgment and intuition.

Significant Effects. By what principles are "significant" policy effects to be distinguished from "insignificant" ones? A number of technical rules have been applied, but these are open to serious objection. The everyday rules of social research and of science by which significance is determined may not always be suitable for use in policy evaluation. The following are examples of challenges to these conventionalisms:

1. *Social work.* One critic has argued that the results of experimentation on social casework can be interpreted in only one way: casework has failed (Fischer, 1973). Another review of the same body of research has shown that most studies are insensitive to anything less than very large effects. Further, the definition of significant effects and the probability of detecting them had been determined by arbitrary technical rules of thumb.

Sizes of effects and experimental sensitivity are philosophical issues that cannot be settled by the use of technical rules. Therefore, it was asserted, no conclusive test had yet been conducted (Crane, 1976).

2. *Public health.* In 1978 the commissioner of health of the state of New York issued a report containing evidence, he claimed, of significant effects on human health of exposure to buried chemical wastes (Whalen et al., 1978). The report cited a number of health effects, including substantially increased rates of miscarriages and birth defects. Subsequently, a scientific review panel dismissed these findings as inconclusive, owing to the small size of the samples and the lack of a comparable control group (Thomas and Associates, 1980). After reviewing both sets of evidence, a noted epidemiologist attacked the conclusions of the review panel and argued that the samples were adequate to the problem at hand and that the controls exceeded normal standards of epidemiological research (Bross, 1980). This argument hinged on appropriate standards of evidence in the public policy realm: the traditional skepticism of science versus the inability of public policy making to wait indefinitely on scientifically conclusive evidence. (A more detailed treatment of the Love Canal case is given in Chapter 12.)

Uncertain Inferences

Measurements are subject to variations that are due both to the inaccuracy of measuring devices and to changes over time in the variables being measured. Evaluation in even the simplest cases, therefore, involves inferences. Since there is often a body of past experience showing the relative frequency with which data patterns will be observed, these inferences need not be mere guesses. In such cases it is often possible to plan the evaluation so as to make use of the laws of probability in drawing inferences. In other cases information about populations is too scarce to allow the use of probability theory, and nonprobabilistic forms of inference must be employed. Most evaluations require the use of both the probabilistic and nonprobabilistic forms.

The use of probabilistic inference involves coming to terms with a vast and controversial statistical literature. In this study treatment of the more technical issues is reserved for Part III (Chapters 8–12). Policy issues can be subsumed under three broad topics:

1. *Values and random uncertainty.* Random uncertainty is controllable by the use of decision rules and sampling and measurement procedures required by the rules. Conventional decision rules exist, but their adequacy for evaluation problems is in dispute. For example, it is often questioned whether conventional null hypotheses and the .05 and .01 levels of significance are adequate (Morrison and Henkel, 1970; Crane, 1976). If they are not, then how should type 1 and type 2 errors be determined — by technical or philosophical principles?

2. *Fluctuating policy variables.* Populations from which samples are drawn are conventionally assumed to have fixed parameters (e.g., means, proportions, and differences in these quantities). Evaluations frequently sample from dynamic systems of variables with fluctuating parameters, not collections of fixed objects. Two problems arise: how to take account of the fluctuations and how to combine the results of successive inferences over time.

3. *Plausibility of possible findings.* What is generally at issue in evaluations is the relative plausibility of a range of possible findings. Rarely is evaluation so precise as to reduce these to one or two. But as yet there is no definition and measure of relative plausibility that is generally accepted for use in policy evaluation. Similar policy issues arise around nonprobabilistic inference.

Scientists' and Citizens' Roles

If issues can be turned into technical problems of research design, they may be dealt with by scientists; otherwise scientists can make no special claim to be entrusted with them. The line between technical decisions and policy judgments is often difficult to draw. This is true even in cases in which the determination of outcomes rests on highly specialized knowledge. Determining acceptable effects of low-level radiation is a problem of this type. The technical task is to measure the relationship of exposure to risk. But when scientists, as currently, are unable to choose between competing models of this relationship, they employ a traditional scientific rule: choose the simplest model (Rotblat, 1981, p. 34). This rule was devised to serve the needs of science; it is not self-evident that it is also an optimum rule for public policy making. In some cases this rule might lead to extremely "safe" policies; in others, to extremely "risky" ones. But who should judge the safety and risk? Should the choice of model in such cases be left entirely to the scientists, or should there be an independent analysis of the data for purposes of policy evaluation? Allowing nonscientists an important role in making judgments will not make the task easier. Procedures that can be defended as valid and just must be identified. Unfortunately, no current approach to evaluation deals exhaustively with this problem.

Many evaluation problems cross the boundaries of natural and social science and the humanities (Shrader-Frechette, 1980). Largely as an accident of history, natural scientists have tended to be involved mainly in evaluations of risks to human well-being, and social scientists in social program evaluation. As argued in the Introduction, these two realms of evaluation are more closely interrelated than their present separation suggests. The debate between Doub and Shrader-Frechette, cited above, is in part a reflection of differing views as to the appropriate disciplines to be involved in public policy on nuclear power.

We now turn to a more detailed comparison of approaches to policy evaluation, making use of the schema outlined in this chapter.

2 EVALUATION AND SOCIAL RESEARCH

EVALUATION AS SCIENTIFIC THEORY TESTING

Evaluation and Social Inquiry

In this approach the problem of evaluation is converted into a problem of testing scientific hypotheses. For example, evaluation of a guaranteed annual income policy is turned into a test of an economic hypothesis about labor force participation. In such applications the assumption is made that the needs of science and those of policy making are parallel.

A case can be made, for example, that economics has power to explain criminal recidivism. From the economic explanations, hypotheses concerning measures effective in the control of recidivism can be derived. In more detail, this argument rests on the claim that economics has something to say about any institution in which constrained choices are made — that is, choices of scarce means to achieve alternative ends (Rottenberg, 1973). Given the scarcity of the means, the choices are costly; part of the cost is the forgone uses to which the means might have been put. Economics provides maximizing choice principles — that is, principles that offer the best hope of achieving desired ends. These principles apply only to groups of decision makers, not to individuals. The individual serves the theory mainly as an analytical or didactic device, a building block in the construction of propositions about the behavior of aggregates.

A most important postulate of this theory is that the decision makers behave rationally. This means that in making choices, account is taken both of the prospective gains and costs, and that the choices made can be shown to have more favorable prospects than any others that could have been made.

The assumption of rationality is not meant to be tested. Together with other elements of the decision-making scheme, it is intended simply as a source of hypotheses. If testing these hypotheses proves to be fruitful, the theory has its uses. For example, the postulate of economic rationality was used to plan an experimental program of aid to released prisoners (Mallar and Thornton, 1978). From the postulate it was deduced that recidivism could be lessened by changing its associated rewards and costs. This could be accomplished either by enhancing the rewards for legitimate activities or by increasing expected punishment for criminal behavior.

The former option was selected. Financial grants were made to newly released prisoners during the transitional period following release. Prior studies documenting that resources of prisoners are generally slim and welfare generally unavailable were the basis for predicting that the financial aid would make a difference. In Baltimore, 432 released prisoners, considered to be at high risk of committing theft crimes but with no known history of alcoholism or narcotic addiction, were selected as the study population. This population was randomly divided into four groups. The first group received $60 a week for three months and job placement services for up to one year following release. The second group received only the financial aid, and the third group only the job placement services. The fourth group received neither treatment. After one year the recidivism rates of the groups receiving financial aid were 26 percent lower than for the other two groups. Thus the use of economic theory to guide further experimentation was supported.

In this particular case it was possible to put the hypotheses to an experimental test. In many important areas of evaluation, however, this is impractical. Thus, to study the effects of low levels of radiation on the probability of developing leukemia and other forms of cancer, secondary sources of data must be used. The amount of available data is insufficient to permit a conclusive test. Researchers recently found that three models of the relationship between exposure to low-level radiation and probability of leukemia fit available data equally well (Rotblat, 1981). By one of the three models, the effects of low-level radiation are from four to six times as great as by another.

This problem of choosing between models arises in a number of areas, such as the effects of exposure to lead (Collingridge, 1981) and vinyl chloride (Brown, 1979). In the scientific approach to evaluation, such uncertainties are resolved by appealing to the conventions or traditions of the particular sciences involved.

Valuation

In the scientific approach, science is more than a method. It is the principal source of values to guide — or, more accurately, to permeate — the inquiry. The following values are especially influential: objectivity, impartiality, accuracy, precision, replication, prediction, and control. Evaluators are expected to become committed to these values and to keep any personal value commitments from influencing the findings and interpretations. Guarding against such influence is one of the functions of research design and of the rules of procedural validity.

Value judgments made in standard contexts may form the content of the inquiry as in consumer opinion studies. Value judgments in "ideal contexts" — that is, assertions as to what is valuable on the whole and in the long run — are sharply limited and, if possible, eliminated entirely. An effort is made to turn questions involving value judgments — "ought" questions — into factual questions, one way being to restrict the inquiry to values on which there is consensus, such as cost and efficiency. Other values are treated as being outside the scope of evaluation research; these values, it is held, must be settled in the political realm, thus enabling the problem of evaluation to be hinged entirely on questions of fact (Collingridge, 1981).

Recall in Chapter 1 that exclusion of values from the inquiry was a feature of the income maintenance experiments. The variable, "marital dissolution rate," was included in the experiment; the interpretation of the finding of an increased rate, however, was restricted to an assessment of its implications for program costs. No other value judgment on this variable was permitted. A similar restriction was placed on the interpretation of findings on labor force participation of women. Using this exclusion device, plus restricting the evaluation to essentially factual questions, avoids explicit conflicts among values that enter into the inquiry.

Values and Observations

Since the content of measures is determined by theoretical considerations, values play little or no part in their creation. Converting evaluation into a problem of explanation from which values have been largely excluded eliminates the need for value scaling. The only need for rescaling of outcome data is to convert data where possible into monetary units, for benefit/cost analysis.

To decide on effect sizes to be taken as significant, several devices are employed:

1. *An appeal to technical rules or procedures.* In the study of the effects of low-level radiation on health noted earlier (Rotblat, 1981), scientists employed the criterion of statistical significance to decide whether observed data departed from their models.

2. *An appeal to "natural" standards.* Radiation emissions from nuclear installations are commonly considered to be insignificant if, by standard measures, they are less than natural background radiation.

3. *What has been found in previous research.* In educational experimentation, the effect of an experimental variable is commonly looked on as significant if it exceeds a fixed proportion of the overall standard deviation (Novick and Jackson, 1974, p. 24). This is based on previous research showing that effects of this order are what have generally been achieved in the past.

4. *An appeal to the argument from ignorance.* For example, if there is no known case of harmful effects from a given level of exposure to lead, this may be taken as a safe level. Collingridge recounts a case in which a "safe" threshold was derived from the work of one highly respected researcher working with samples of adult males. The standard was unquestioningly applied to determine safe levels of exposure for children, the rationale being that there is no known case of lead poisoning from exposures below the threshold. Subsequently, it was discovered that the threshold was too high for children (Collingridge, 1981, p. 191). Another very common argument, based on ignorance, is the one that "there is no known case of a fatality resulting from low-level radiation" (Shrader-Frechette, 1980, p. 55).

Uncertain Inferences

Evaluation as applied science makes use of the rules of procedural validity that govern science itself. The proceedings are rather like a court: instead of specifying in advance what constitutes "truth" in every conceivable case, a set of procedural rules that promise to minimize uncertainty over the long run is followed (compare the procedural justice concept discussed in Rawls, 1972, pp. 83–85). A basic rule is that acceptance or rejection of findings should be based on preestablished impersonal criteria (Edsall, 1981, p. 11). Findings must be publicly presented, preferably after critical review by peers. Reports must indicate limits of uncertainty of findings and inferences; they must also appropriately acknowledge indebtedness to the work of other scientists, published and unpublished.

The entire system of review is one of "organized skepticism": every effort is made to disconfirm findings. A false positive is looked on as a more serious error than a false negative. Consequently, the rules are weighted in favor of rejection or at least suspension of decision. Validity of peer review rests on an assumed consensus among scientists in a given field about where the line between acceptance and rejection should be drawn. "Stringency" varies widely in different fields (Edsall, 1981, p. 11). In physics, Popper recommends that acceptable deviations from a proposed model be defined by the limits of measurement precision (Popper, 1965, p. 201). This standard is extremely stringent. In genetics Edwards recommends a considerably wider band of tolerated uncertainty (Edwards, 1972, p. 182).

Roles of Scientists and Lay Persons in Evaluation

A sharp distinction is made between the evaluator's role as citizen and as scientist. In the latter role the emphasis is on impartial inquiry; in the former it is to speak out after the inquiry is completed. A vital role is assigned to scientific peers of the evaluator. They are responsible for review and criticism at each stage and for a final review before findings are released. Lay persons have no special role in the evaluation; their use of the evaluation is in the political realm only.

LIMITATIONS OF THE SCIENTIFIC
THEORY-TESTING APPROACH

In basic science the rules of procedural validity have become increasingly difficult to apply as the financial stakes and other stakes in science have become greater (Edsall, 1981, p. 12). When scientists are asked to make judgments on public policy issues, such rules can hardly be applied at all. In this field no well-established consensus exists among scientists as to the grounds for rejection of hypotheses.

The degree to which conservatism and skepticism should be guides is often disputed; these terms have uncertain meanings when applied to policy decisions. In basic science a finding can be kept out of the body of accepted knowledge until there is consensus that it can neither be disconfirmed nor ignored. This conservative tactic (an appeal to the argument based on ignorance) serves to prevent science from having its corpus of knowledge cluttered with false positives.

In the policy realm, the advantages of this tactic are far less obvious. A 100 percent increase in the rate of miscarriages may have to be accepted as real, without waiting for final word from basic science, which may be many years in coming. Even then the import of the message may be in doubt.

An important example of this uncertainty can be seen in the scientific estimates on the effects of low-level radiation on health; these estimates have very recently been called into serious question (Rotblat, 1981); a series of revisions have occurred over the last thirty years. It is hardly practical for public policy making to echo these ups and downs, but it has not yet worked out its own rules of evidence or what to do in cases of scientific uncertainty.

The weakness of social science generalizations, coupled with the stringent conventional standards of evidence usually applied, leads to a large conservative bias (examined further in Chapter 11). Equivocality of findings leads to delay in policy making or excessive caution: "You can't solve problems by throwing money at them," as Richard Nixon argued (Aaron, 1978, p. 33).

The attempt to reduce evaluation to factual statements, whether quantitative or narrative, leads to a contradiction: value-free evaluation. Clearly, personal value judgments are inappropriate, but characterizing judgments (Nagel, 1961, pp. 492-93), as well as judgments in standard and ideal contexts (Kaplan, 1964, p. 396), are not only appropriate but also required. To omit values such as equity because there is debate over their meaning simplifies but also may impoverish the findings, a theme developed later in this chapter and in Chapter 3.

EVALUATION AS APPLIED SCIENTIFIC METHODS

Evaluation and Social Inquiry

Because scientific explanations especially in the social sciences, are both scarce and uncertain, most evaluation problems are in practice reduced to applications of social research methodology. This renders the problem of evaluation both familiar and tractable, and enables social scientists to make use of the research skills in which they were trained. Evidence suggests that experts in evaluation assign a high priority to skills in quantitative methods (Anderson and Ball, 1978).

Evaluation as scientific methodology is a close relative of the applied science approach from which it emerged. Its stance on the place of values in evaluation, the relationship of values to data, and the roles of scientist and citizen is essentially the same as in the scientific approach. The major difference from the applied science approach is in the framing of evaluation questions in scientific methodology. These are intended not to test scientific theory but to provide a rigorous test of net effects of a policy. To this end, as Rossi, Freeman, and Wright (1979) point out, the basic approaches to producing reliable and valid evidence, which have evolved in the social sciences, are employed (p. 31). The ideal characteristics of social evaluation in this tradition are replicability (others should be able to repeat the evaluation in the same way), the introduction of tests of whether the effects of policies would have occurred under alternative policies, and the collection of evidence as to the efficient use of resources.

Valuation

The most important value in decision making is realism — that is, basing decisions on hard evidence. Realism demands a rigorous assessment of the degree to which policies and programs accomplish their primary missions (Rossi, Freeman, and Wright, 1979, p. 20). The special importance attached to rigorous assessment may derive from science or from the perspective of the federal decision maker who wishes to ensure that public funds are well spent. It also stems from a widespread impression that all too often social programs are misguided, badly implemented, and ineffective (Rossi, Freeman, and Wright, 1979, p. 20). Thus the most important values to be applied to policies are *effectiveness* and *efficiency*, values that require four types of evaluative questions to be addressed:

1. *Program-planning questions*: the extent and distribution of target populations; conformity of program design to policy goals.
2. *Monitoring policy implementation*: actual versus intended services; the extent to which intended populations are being reached by service.
3. *Impact assessment*: effectiveness in achieving goals; ruling out alternative explanations of policy effects.
4. *Economic efficiency questions*: cost-effectiveness; ratios of benefits to costs.

Methods

The first two types of questions call for the use of quantitative descriptive methods: statistical description (Spiegel, 1961, chapters 1–5), measures of association (Spiegel, 1961, chapters 14, 15), as well as estimation and hypothesis testing (Spiegel, 1961, chapters 9, 10). The third type requires the use of experimental or quasi-experimental designs (Cook and Campbell, 1976). The fourth type, economic efficiency questions, is most demanding methodologically; so that costs of outcomes can be related to benefits, outcomes must be commensurable. If only some outcomes are commensurable, the others must be combinable in such a way as to create a commensurable set. The consequences — both immediate and long term — of possible actions to be evaluated must be measurable. Direction of causation must be clear. The effects of extraneous variables must be known or at least controllable. Benefits must be exhaustively catalogued, and there must be agreement among evaluators as to the relative importance of different benefits and how these benefits are related to any harmful outcomes that might also occur.

These conditions are most easily satisfied in such decisions as locating a manufacturing plant, planning an airport, and building a road. (For discussion of these and more complex examples, see Thompson, 1980.) The extent to which they are applicable in risk assessment and in the evaluation of social programs is a current topic of debate that will be more fully discussed in Chapter 3 (see also Bupp, 1979, p. 145).

Values and Data

Measures seldom are converted into value scales by any formal process. Rather, they are structured to reflect policy and program goals determined by prior studies addressed to the needs of "target" populations and by consultation with policy makers and program managers. A definition of significant effects may be arrived at in any of the following ways:

1. *Comparative benefit/cost ratios*: Differences in ratios that are large enough to make a practical difference to budgets are viewed as significant.
2. *Judgments of the social worth of policy effects*: Small effects are considered to be important if worth is high, and conversely (Rossi, Freeman, and Wright, 1979, p. 241).

3. *Relevance to policy makers*: Goals being tested should be chosen and formulated in the light of policy makers' concerns; these should be fully ascertained in advance (Rossi, Freeman, and Wright, 1979, p. 241).

Uncertain Inferences

The issue of generalization of findings is typically expressed as a problem of balancing *internal validity* — the capability of an evaluation to estimate net effects — against *external validity* — the ability to generalize soundly beyond the samples tested. External validity is considered important. Therefore, representative samples should be carefully chosen, a comparatively straightforward requirement when samples are made up of persons chosen from enumerable lists. Much more complicated sampling designs are required in cases in which the sampling units are communities, schools, clinics, or other organizations (Rossi, Freeman, and Wright, 1979, chapter 3).

Related to the problem of internal and external validity is the need to balance type 1 and type 2 errors. Prevailing practice in quantitative methodological evaluations is reliance on conventionalism — the use of the .05 and .01 levels of significance. The prevalence of this practice is documented in Chapter 11.

Scientist and Citizen

Competence in evaluation calls for professional preparation in social science. Evaluation has a specialized vocabulary, shorthand expressions, and procedures (Rossi, Freeman, and Wright, 1979, p. 29). The techniques of quantitative evaluation, in particular, are highly complex and sophisticated in application, to be employed only by highly trained specialists. There is little room for the citizen in these activities. On the other hand, a number of roles in evaluation are best performed by the nonspecialist: the policy maker, program sponsor, evaluation sponsor, the person served, program managers and staff, and interest groups (p. 294). The following principles will facilitate cooperation among the participants (p. 245):

1. Shared understanding of the project.
2. Clarity of goals: common understanding of goals.

3. Automony of evaluators: This doesn't always require that the evaluators be outsiders. Program planning and monitoring questions can be evaluated effectively by members of the organizations in which programs are implemented.

4. Allowing adequate lead time: This can be facilitated by planning for evaluation at the early stages of policy development and implementation or at points at which policy changes are contemplated.

THE APPLIED SCIENTIFIC METHODS APPROACH: A CRITIQUE

The applied scientific methods approach not only has been popular but also immensely productive. Evidence of its productivity includes the rapid advances in modeling change and response uncertainty made in recent years, with corresponding increases in the sensitivity and power of evaluation (Tuma and Robins, 1980); the increasingly sophisticated methods of time series analysis (McCleary and Hay, 1980); and the rapid development of research on multiequation models (Duncan, 1975). A number of newer methods provide powerful alternatives to experimental designs (Jöreskog and Sörbom, 1979; Magidson, 1977). Undoubtedly rapid progress will continue, aided by similar developments in statistics and computer technology.

As a structure for policy evaluation, quantitative methodology has a number of limitations, many of which also limit the scientific approach. Especially important are the logical flaws of naturalism — the effort to reduce "ought" statements to "is" statements — mentioned earlier in this chapter. In addition, the following general limitations are noted:

1. A welter of quantitative methodologies with no clear basis for choosing among them exists and may, in fact, lead to choices based on the evaluator's methodological preferences rather than the demands of the problem. As is often asserted, the problem should preface the method.

2. The scientific methodology approach offers limited guidance on the context and scope of valuation, values and measures, problems of uncertainty, and scientists' and citizens' roles.

3. On close analysis evaluations stemming from apparently value-free methodologies can be shown to rest on complex value judgments. This has been nicely demonstrated by House in his critique of the well-known study of equality of educational opportunity by Coleman and Associates (House, 1980, p. 132). A recent study of decision

making in the field of nuclear energy shows that experts' predictions of future uranium resources are closely correlated with their judgments of the worthwhileness of taking the risks of nuclear proliferation. The researchers interpret this to mean that the experts' perceptions of "facts" are influenced by their global value judgments on the larger issues in public policy on nuclear power (Manne and Richels, 1980).

4. Free-floating, inexplicit value judgments inevitably collide, a problem that can be dealt with only by the application of some priority rule among values. If value assessments are implicit, however, no priority rule can be applied. Consequently, unrecognized priorities may be applied.

5. In the scientific approach to evaluation, the importance of findings lies in the implications for science. The test of a scientific theory is generally regarded as important in its own right. Evaluations based primarily on methodology cannot offer this justification. Consequently, the findings of such studies have frequently been attacked as trivial (e.g., by Cronbach and Associates, 1980). A common argument advanced by these critics is that, if policy makers pay little attention to quantitative outcomes, these are seldom worth the effort needed to produce them (Cronbach and Associates, 1980, p. 127). Those who approach evaluation as a form of social change or social action consultation attempt to avoid this problem by placing the evaluator close to the action as it unfolds. Being fully aware of the information needs of different actors at different stages of policy development, the evaluator is in a better position to see that the findings are used. This will rescue evaluation from the problem of triviality.

The merits of this last argument are further examined later. It seems clear, however, that taking the wants of policy makers as given may not always be sufficient. Some independent assessment of these wants may be needed.

THE PROBLEM OF NATURALISM IN EVALUATION

In both of the scientific approaches to policy evaluation an effort is made, as we have seen, to minimize, if not eliminate, need for value judgments. To this end, all values are excluded from the analysis except those about which there is little dispute. Alternatively, judgments such as acceptability or significance may be based on purely technical rules. This amounts to deriving values from facts, as can be seen in the following examples:

1. *Equating the morally acceptable with the statistically insignificant.* In the Rasmussen and Bethe reports on nuclear power (see Chapter 3 and Shrader-Frechette, 1980, p. 139), a morally acceptable increase in the number of cancer deaths is defined as a statistically insignificant increase. In accordance with this principle, a proposal to dispose of nuclear waste off the British coastline is held to be morally acceptable because it will lead to only a 1.66 percent annual increase in cancer deaths. This increase is statistically insignificant. On the basis of this rule, a risk of 5,000 deaths from a nuclear accident is also considered to be acceptable. The same principle is employed in social services evaluation. A statistically significant difference is taken to be significant for policy making; conversely, a statistically insignificant difference is held to be insignificant for this purpose. This is the almost universal practice, as shown in Chapter 11. Statistically insignificant effects are also said to be satisfactorily explained by chance.

2. *Equating the morally acceptable with what occurs in nature.* The commonly used standard of acceptability of exposure to man-made radiation is the level of natural background radiation; the same reasoning is applied to other pollutants, such as noise, lead, and food additives (Lowrance, 1976, p. 85).

3. *Equating the morally acceptable with what has previously been accepted.* This principle is commonly used in setting occupational safety standards (Lowrance, 1976, p. 85).

The appeal to natural standards of values is open to several sorts of serious objections, including the following.

The Naturalistic Fallacy

According to Shrader-Frechette (1980), most philosophers agree that derivations of values from facts are logically fallacious. Some view them also as a form of moral blindness (Shrader-Frechette, 1980, p. 160).

Arbitrariness

Whatever view we take of the naturalistic fallacy, it is apparent that the attempt to base values on facts leads to judgments that are both arbitrary and inconsistent. Whether an increase in cancer deaths, for example, is statistically significant is mainly determined by the existing rate plus a number of fortuitous factors. To decide that an increase of 5,000 cancer deaths is morally acceptable because it is statistically insignificant is merely to assert that with the existing high incidence of cancer, human life is cheap. Apart from its moral blindness, this assumption overlooks the epidemiological studies that show that the so-called "natural" base rate of cancer used as a standard of acceptability may in itself be a product of hazards created by the petrochemical and other industries.

Confusion of Description with Explanation

In social service evaluation, a statistically insignificant finding is interpreted to mean that the observed effects are sufficiently explained by chance. For two reasons, however, this interpretation is ambiguous. First, a statistically significant finding may or may not be significant in an evaluative sense. In its common usage the term "significant" means "of real importance," "weighty," or "substantial." But statistically significant means none of these things: it means only "rare" — that is, less often than once in twenty (or once in a hundred) times. Consequently, a result that is so small as to be inconsequential for evaluation purposes may be statistically significant. Conversely, a result that is large enough to be of great importance for social evaluation may not be statistically significant.

Second, the phrase "sufficiently explained by chance," as used in routine statistical inference, means nothing more than "consistent with a hypothesis." Since a result that is consistent with a null hypothesis may also be consistent with an infinity of other hypotheses, acceptance of a null hypothesis constitutes no explanation in the usual sense of this term. To explain an event is to account for it — that is, to show that necessary and sufficient conditions for the occurrence of the event have been satisfied.

The laws of chance provide no explanation of events in the sense that physical laws provide explanations; they are merely descriptive. Results that are in accord with a statistical null hypothesis may be much more in need of explanation than results that contradict the hypothesis. The phrase "sufficiently explained by chance," therefore, is misleading and should not be employed.

Confusion of Policy Decisions with Technical Decisions

The statistical significance or insignificance of a research finding is determined in part by the degree of uncertainty the evaluator is prepared to accept. This problem is a policy problem, not a technical issue; it hinges on the judgment of the importance to society of effects that are small in magnitude. In contrast, purely technical issues can often be dealt with by rules of thumb or by an appeal to magic numbers, such as .05.

EVALUATION AS DIRECTED SOCIAL CHANGE

Evaluation and Social Inquiry

To many researchers a more compelling model for policy evaluation than either science or research technology is planned social change, an event brought about by changing the perceptions and attitudes of individual participants in the process. As these persons are guided through a process of systematic examination of programs and policies, their perceptions of policies change and their energies for action are mobilized. Therein lies the real power of evaluation.

This theme has a number of variations, such as utilization-focused evaluation (Patton, 1980), the case study approach (Stake, 1978), and evaluation as education (Cronbach and Associates, 1980).

Utilization-Focused Evaluation

Patton's work on utilization-focused evaluation stresses the personal factor in change — that is, the need to get information into the hands of those persons who are interested enough to act on it. This is the best if not the only way of ensuring that the evaluation will have impact.

Valuation. Patton makes no distinction among different contexts of valuation. All valuation is treated as "personal." A major weight is to be given to the values of decision makers. The evaluator's own values, on the other hand, are downplayed.

Evaluation must above all be useful. It must, therefore, be directed at persons who really care — persons who can use information, to whom information makes a difference, who have questions they want to have answered, and who care about and are willing to share responsibility for the evaluation and its utilization (Patton, 1980, p. 284).

A workable number of these persons (ideally between five and ten) should be recruited to exercise a step-by-step supervison of the evaluation. It is the felt needs of this group, often taken at face value, that shape the evaluation. The evaluator can still play an active role in the discussion, and point out, if necessary, inconsistencies in the wants and needs. The evaluator works with the task force to find the right questions — that is, questions that are answerable by data, that have more than one possible answer, that need to be answered for the purposes of the decision makers and not for someone else's purposes, and that promise to yield information on which decision makers can act.

Values and Observations. Once evaluation questions have been formulated, possible findings are identified and classified by their desirability (as defined by the task force according to its own lights). To this end it is essential to review the action implications of various possible findings so as to clarify in advance, in a nondefensive atmosphere, the findings that people see as desirable or undesirable.

Uncertain Inferences. Patton's examples are mainly case studies of particular programs. He offers no formal scheme of inference. His general preference seems to be for informal assessments of sample sizes and other factors affecting precision.

Roles of Scientists and Citizens. The set of participants in evaluation is a group of decision makers or information users. In principle, service consumers as well as professionals are included. The evaluator is a resource to the group, but all participants are on an equal footing. Decision makers share in many technical research tasks, such as instrument creation and interpreting factor loadings (Patton, 1980, p. 261).

The evaluator, taking care not to manipulate decision makers to accept preconceived notions of quality research, is more than a mere technician. The change process is one of action, reaction, and adaptation by all group members (Patton, 1980, p. 289). Taking action on findings is the responsibility of individual decision makers and information users.

Evaluation as Education

This point of view is reflected in a recent book by eight members of the Stanford Evaluation Consortium (Cronbach and Associates, 1980). These authors agree with Patton that what matters in evaluation is its effects on the behavior and attitudes of participants and audiences.

Their evaluator, however, is more like an educator and less like a social worker than Patton's. It may be relevant that all eight consortium members have advanced degrees in education, and six are members of educational faculties.

The Evaluator.   Evaluation is a piecemeal adaptation of social policies that proceeds from no fixed ideas of the good social policy or program. The object of the exercise is not to assess goodness but to negotiate improvements, one step at a time (Cronbach and Associates, 1980, p. 66). In the process, the evaluator offers evidence and ideas pertinent to pending actions, thus helping the participants to think more clearly and to be better informed. A close parallel can be drawn between the evaluator's behavior and that of the ideal educator (Cronbach and Associates, pp. 160–63).

The "classroom" is the PSC — the policy-shaping community. The PSC is made up of legislators, policy makers, program administrators, operating personnel, illuminators (e.g., journalists and other outside observers), and constituencies (e.g., citizens' lobbies). The evaluator works with members of the PSC to identify problems that are ripe for evaluation, to negotiate questions to be studied, to obtain political support, and to select appropriate measures and patterns of observation. Choosing variables to observe requires intimate, first-hand observation by the evaluator. A variety of sources must be consulted, and methods must be flexible.

Evaluators must probe for unavowed as well as avowed goals and for a sensible evaluation charter that contains realistic expectations of research. Questions must be answerable. If necessary, evaluators can even help with the decision to abort a project. Such a situation may occur if it becomes apparent that a program exists only on paper. The key role of the evaluator is to serve as a link among various persons in the PSC.

It is often better to launch a series of small studies than one ambitious one. As findings begin to come in, they should be released bit by bit over an extended period of time. There should be different reports for different consumers, with formats being varied to suit the audience. A variety of media should be employed. Massive one-shot final reports should, for the most part, be avoided. For many audiences, stories are better than statistics.

Evaluators should monitor and pursue implementation actively; their work is not finished when the study report is done. Rather, with findings in hand, they should continue to engage the PSC, a move that often involves sharing the actions of one set of community members with another. Unlike Patton, the consortium takes explicit account of the possibility that members of the PSC will take various partisan points of view on the evaluation. Herein lies the distinctive role of the evaluator, who is impartial — that is, able to see the program through the eyes of diverse partisans. Care must be taken not to pose questions in such a way as to favor the interests of one agency, one sector of society, or the evaluator's own ideology. An adequate evaluation plan contains questions that arise from all partisans. In striving for openness and neutrality, in shaping techniques to bring both good and bad news to light, and in making interpretations that consider the facts from conflicting perspectives, evaluators can be "multipartisans" or "public scientists."

Valuation.   Like Patton, the consortium applies values to evaluations, not to policies and programs. For evaluations, the supreme value is service to society (Cronbach and Associates, 1980, p. 65). Evaluation must contribute to the political processes by which policies are shaped. To do this, it must enlighten.

A second important value is impartiality. The evaluator should serve, as we have seen, the needs of all stakeholders, even when they are in conflict. The evaluator is an obvious echo of the disinterested observer of utilitarianism who integrates the wants of all participants into a coherent whole (Rawls, 1972, p. 27).

Uncertain Inferences.   An important contribution of this work is the effort made to clarify the scope of inference in evaluation. It is pointed out that three distinct sets of inferences are always required (Cronbach and Associates, 1980, p. 233):

1.   From u to U: from units sampled to population units.
2.   From t to T: from treatments applied in a particular experiment to all the possible realizations of the treatments.
3.   From o to O: from the particular measures employed to the population of all relevant measures.

Most inferences in practice are not from a uto to a well-defined UTO but to a $*UTO$, in which one or more of U, T, and O differs from the UTO. Such inferences can seldom, if ever, be modeled statistically.

The Qualitative Case Study Approach

This approach differs from the preceding two in insisting on the use of qualitative methods of data collection and observation. One finds, however, the same emphasis on getting close to the communities for which the evaluation is intended to be useful. A leading proponent (Stake, 1978, p. 5) argues that findings must be presented in ways that are in harmony with the reader's experiences. If this is done, findings will be felt as a natural ground for generalization. Being similar to the studies carried out by practitioners, which are complex, holistic, and focused on personal meanings, case studies are more likely to affect practice than hypothesis tests and statistics. Moreover, because of their flexible structures, case studies can more easily be responsive to the needs of different audiences. The importance attached to this quality by Stake is indicated by his referring to his approach as "responsive evaluation."

Valuation. All efforts to restrict in advance the variables to be studied or the value perspectives to be adopted are to be deplored. As in utilization-focused evaluation, values are considered to be personal. Valuation rests on shared meanings but is an idiosyncratic, personal experience. Idiosyncracy is itself highly valued. Evaluations must be designed to capture differences in meanings and wants; this is the main object of the exercise. The evaluative study can become an examination of how the workings of a social policy are experienced by the different persons affected by it (Lofland, 1971, p. 7; Stake, 1978, p. 6; Wilson, 1979, p. 448; Filstead, 1981).

Advocates of the case study approach seem primarily interested in the values associated with the case study itself. The most important of these are as follows:

1. *Particularism.* The goal is to portray in detail the events in a particular situation. The researcher proceeds inductively, attempting to understand the situation without imposing preestablished categories of observation or experimental conditions. Patterns emerge from the unstructured observations only at an advanced stage of the research; theories are emergent and local, grounded in observation. Both the individuals and the programs studied are considered to be unique, thus findings of parallel studies at different sites are not expected to be the same although much can be learned by comparing them (Wilson, 1979; Patton, 1980, pp. 40–41).

2. *Holism.* An effort is made to capture as many dimensions as possible — a tactic that often requires looking at histories and broad environments. To be holistic is to portray the dynamics of the case, the interplay of factors and forces. Typically, evaluations cover a period of time over which they recount the unfolding and interplay of events (Wilson, 1979; Patton, 1980, p. 41).

3. *Value neutrality and pluralism.* Emphasis is placed on describing the event or the scene just as it is, without the imposition of value judgments or the bias of researchers; this helps to ensure that the meanings of the situation as felt by the participants will come through. Equally important, the reader of the evaluation will be taken into the setting and will be able to apprehend the situation as it is, not as screened through the researchers' conceptual apparatus (Patton, 1980, p. 36).

4. *Completeness.* Proponents of the case study approach hold that the case study omits less than any other form of evaluation. Therefore, they argue, it is the most adequate form, not only for its immediate audience, but also for other evaluators who will find in case study reports enough information to carry out similar studies in other settings (Wilson, 1979, p. 446).

Uncertain Inferences. The insistence on the use of qualitative methods rules out the use of formal schemes of statistical inference or any other use of probability theory. Stake holds that immersion in particular situations will in time make clear to the researcher their recurrent interconnections and natural covariations. He refers to the recognition of these patterns as "natural generalization" (Stake, 1978, p. 6). This he holds is both intuitive and empirical. Being based on events as they actually occur, and not as artificially restructured by the researcher, naturalistic generalizations are more valid than statistical generalizations.

Other writers on the case study approach have emphasized the particularity, so to speak, of the generalizations appropriate for evaluations —that is, their difference from scientific laws. What is sought, after all, is information about actions in local contexts, carried out by small numbers of decision makers. Evaluations are always caught up in a historical time and place. Generalizations crumble. The goal of unassailable certainty is inappropriate and must be given up. Evaluators could be of much more use to decision makers if they aimed to provide perspectives and illuminations rather than hard findings (Parlett and Hamilton, 1976, p. 144; Patton, 1980, pp. 282-83).

Scientists and Citizens. The qualitative case study has flowered in recent years in the fields of personal social services, such as special education, family therapy, mental health, outdoor recreation, community nursing and casework with the handicapped, the urban elderly, foster children, alcoholics, parolees, and nursing patients (for a bibliography of studies see Filstead, 1981, pp. 266-67). The typical research consumer is the professional providing one of these services. The evaluation serves the professional as a means of "feedback" from persons directly served and from other persons and agencies involved in the program.

The evaluator is primarily a facilitator of communication, a clarifier both of shared meanings and of differences in perception. A commonly employed method of the evaluator is to bring in a series of outside observers of the service, each of whom offers a unique perspective on it (Stake, 1978, p. 6). As in utilization-focused evaluation, the views of all participants count equally. Evaluators have no special authority or claims to objectivity deriving from their competence in research methodology. Roles in the group of participants are differentiated not by this kind of competence but by the different types of information required by different actors.

The art of preparing reports (written or verbal) to respond to these different needs is an important theme in the literature of the case study (Wilson, 1979). Although no sharp distinction is made between scientist and citizen, major attention in practice seems to be given to meeting the needs of service professionals — the most active consumers of information. Citizens are more often in the role of subjects to be observed and suppliers of information. In other words, they have no special role in the conduct of the evaluation.

LIMITATIONS OF EVALUATION
AS DIRECTED SOCIAL CHANGE

Linking evaluation questions to program decision making and clinical practice is one way of endowing them with significance. Concentrating the evaluation on variables that have political leverage is another means to this end (Cronbach and Associates, 1980, p. 265). But leverage depends mainly on political power. Evaluations that are self-consciously designed to have leverage will almost inevitably cater to established powers: to employers rather than unorganized workers; to proponents of large-scale strategies rather than decentralized energy strategies. Preoccupation with leverage would have led Rachel Carson to consult the chemical industry in advance about its possible reception of her proposed study.

Leverage can also be thought of as the market value of information: the probability that "consumers" will "buy" it, what it is worth to them. The evaluator becomes an entrepreneur, aiming a product at an identifiable market sector. The value of the product depends on the views of the customers; what the evaluator might be able to contribute on this point matters a good deal less.

One strength of the social change consultation approaches to evaluation lies in the attention that they give to the wants of decision makers and in their sensitivity to the personal factor. These approaches seem especially useful whenever the decision makers can be viewed as a small group of individual buyers of information, each of whom has about equal authority to act. This is often the case in small-scale, internally sponsored evaluations in social agencies and in clinical studies.

On the other hand, a preoccupation with individuals leads evaluators to overlook the role played in policy evaluation by corporate actors (Coleman, 1974). Major issues in policy evaluation today involve such corporate actors as electric power companies, unions, manufacturers' associations, and public utilities. Coleman shows that the emergence of large numbers of these corporate actors has created imbalances of power in society (pp. 55–106). To help right these imbalances, new institutions are needed. Since it may often be able to bring out information that the corporate actors prefer to ignore, policy evaluation can be one of these new institutions; not, however, if it addresses itself only to individual wants and treats the policy-shaping community only as a collection of individuals. In Chapter 3 we turn to evaluation approaches that bring the behavior of large organizations into sharper focus.

A further limitation of the directed social change approach, particularly the case study, is that information about the personal meanings of participation in social programs is of particular interest to clinicians but is irrelevant to the evaluation of many kinds of policy outcomes. The following are examples: being sent to a correctional institution on apparently arbitrary grounds (Gruber, 1980, p. 61); losing one's children to "the welfare" with no opportunity for advance consultation and planning (Neave, 1970); being exposed to serious hazards of the workplace (Gersuny, 1980); or environmental sources of genetic damage (Bross, 1980). Case studies of the subjective meaning of experiencing these risks would at best be preliminary to serious evaluation of policies set up to control them. Larger-scale studies, making use of quantitative data, are called for.

3 EVALUATION AND SOCIAL JUSTICE

A UTILITARIAN PERSPECTIVE ON POLICY EVALUATION

The view of policy evaluation presented in this first section is seldom labeled utilitarian by its proponents. The arguments by which this view is justified, however, amount to an appeal to utilitarian assumptions. Furthermore, these arguments are in conflict with the egalitarian ones presented in the following section. Therefore, classifying the general position as utilitarian seems reasonable.

There are, admittedly, two main versions of utilitarianism: (1) *act utilitarianism* concerns itself with particular acts of individuals and (2) *rule utilitarianism* with the general obligations of agents. We shall accept Lyon's argument that in any case in which an act utilitarian would amend a rule of conduct, a rule utilitarian would have equally good reason to do so (Lyons, 1964). Hence, in the following discussion of policy evaluation, the distinction between these two versions of utilitarianism can be set aside.

Evaluation and Social Inquiry

The utilitarian view of evaluation as a form of inquiry is shaped by several of the major constructs of the utilitarian philosophy. The first is the principle of utility; to conform to this principle, policies must be designed to achieve the greatest possible net balance of good over bad for humankind as a whole. Associated with this principle is the assumption that equality is not an absolute right. Violations of equal rights, such as the disenfranchisement of minorities to serve the good of the majority, may be the lesser of two evils. An overemphasis on equality would slow the pace of economic development and hence reduce the resources available for social welfare.

Disparities in income, for example, may be both natural and beneficial; current social legislation in the United States may have gone too far in the direction of evening out these disparities, resulting in extravagant public sector expenditures and a loss of incentive for individuals to meet their own needs (Anderson, 1980). Government health care programs, for instance, should be sharply reduced so that the free market can substitute less expensive health providers than physicians and dentists. Consumers who wished to accept lower quality care at a reduced price could thus do so. These consumers would then have an incentive to increase their incomes, a pattern that if carried out would benefit everyone (Campbell, 1980, pp. 304-10).

Social provisions in the public sector should be aimed primarily at maximizing economic freedom and opportunity. Individuals are ends in themselves, of supreme value; most are in charge of their own fates. Therefore, social problems such as poverty are accounted for mainly by the characteristics of individuals. Since individuals maximize their utilities, welfare benefits constitute a significant disincentive to work. The way to deal with this problem is to increase the opportunity costs of not working — that is, to ensure that these benefits are available only to those who are disabled from work. Removing all others, even single female heads of families, from the welfare rolls will force them into the labor market and create a new low-income class from which the energetic members will have an incentive and opportunity to rise (Anderson, 1980, pp. 173-74).

In the light of these general concepts, the social services should be focused on the task of bringing members of society who fall behind back into the mainstream as efficiently as possible. The principal role of evaluation is to ensure that the social services are performing this function. Thus evaluation is a tool of policy makers and managers. Its knowledge base is in economics, operations research, and management science. Efficient administration will prevent waste and unnecessary dependency on the state.

Public interest evaluation should encourage self-regulation by industry. Government regulation should be provided only in those areas in which it can demonstrate unequivocally favorable benefit/cost ratios. Where industrial processes involve risks to the public, the response of the public sector should be to inform individuals of the risks so that they can avoid them and in some cases to develop effective treatments for any persons who are harmed. The most efficient mechanism for protecting the environment and human well-being is the price mechanism (Moore, 1980).

Values in Evaluation

Selecting programs for evaluation in the social services should be guided by the need to ensure effectiveness and efficiency and to minimize costs of redistribution programs. Maintaining the principle of less eligibility is also important — that is, welfare rates should be below what can be earned in the lowest paid employment. High-priority programs for evaluation are welfare, personal social services, health, and remedial and compensatory education. Low-priority programs are government regulatory activities, social action, and reform movements.

The values that should be given priority in assessing the outcomes of social services are effectiveness and efficiency. Benefit/cost study receives high priority, and efforts should be made to extend it into new areas. Low priority should be given to equity, inclusiveness, and democratic involvement. The most appropriate measures in evaluation are those that tap individual achievement and social functioning: school achievement tests, scales of social adjustment, measures of earnings.

Significant Effects

The utilitarian emphasis on economic growth requires a concentration of capital on activities held to be economically productive. The greater the rate of growth, the greater the net gain to society and the greater the margin for benevolence. Priority should be given to social programs that are unquestionably cost-effective; these must be programs whose benefits can be translated into monetary units. Since they may divert resources from the all-important goal of economic growth, other kinds of programs require special justification. The onus is clearly on the proponents of such programs to show that they are beneficial; this requires a demonstration of large effects of interventions.

The same argument applies to threats to public safety or health brought about by industrial activities. Since nuclear power, for example, is an essential energy source and potentially a large contributor to growth, a substantial health risk to the population must be demonstrated before constraints or additional costs are imposed on its development. Effect sizes in evaluations must again be substantial.

This argument is frequently advanced in the field of occupational safety. The case study by Brown (1979) of the vinyl chloride industry illustrates how a federal regulatory agency, in response to economic arguments made by manufacturers, reduced its standards of safety below the minimums initially established. This amounts to increasing the size of the health effects of vinyl chloride risk of liver cancer and several other diseases judged as acceptable.

Type 1 and Type 2 Errors

Admittedly, there is some probability of underestimating risks and benefits. Since the social services are considered to play a residual function, concerned mainly with treatment of problems rather than the enhancement of opportunities, and since these services are viewed as a brake on economic growth, it follows that a high degree of protection against type 1 errors should be demanded. That is, there should be little risk of falsely concluding that a social service is effective. This is consistent with one version of the approach to setting type 1 and type 2 errors, originally proposed by Neyman and Pearson (1933): fix type 1 errors at an acceptable level and then seek to minimize type 2 errors to the extent permitted by the research budget. In practice this means that type 2 errors will, in general, be substantially greater than type 1 errors. Since the latter are viewed as more important, this discrepancy is acceptable.

Roles of Scientist and Citizen

Since evaluation is a scientific discipline, citizens have no role in its execution other than the role of information givers.

AN EGALITARIAN PERSPECTIVE

Evaluation and Social Inquiry

In the egalitarian perspective, especially as developed by John Rawls (1972), social policies are to be evaluated primarily by their effects on the basic liberties of the person and by their distributive effects in society. These basic liberties include political liberty, freedom of speech and assembly, liberty of conscience and freedom of thought, freedom of the person, the right to hold personal property, and freedom from arbitrary arrest and seizure

(Rawls, 1972, p. 48). Evaluation is a means of bringing into the open, for critical examination, implicit and far-reaching ethical implications of policies, which, on their surface, appear to have only technical or professional aspects (Shrader-Frechette, 1980, p. 28). Beneath the surface often lies an unacknowledged utilitarian ethical system. The policies suffer from all the limitations of utilitarianism. Evaluation is a means of making these limitations visible, subject to scrutiny. The approach is equally applicable to policies in the industrial and social service realms.

Thus, the egalitarians perceive evaluation to be as much a problem of philosophy as of science. Evaluation must therefore make use of the concepts and methods of philosophical inquiry. Observations are to be interpreted in the light of ethical models as well as scientific ones. For example, the evaluator should ask, What is the implicit paradigm of ethical reasoning in benefit/cost analysis? Probabilistic data are to be viewed as applications of different philosophies of probability, not merely as different methods of calculation.

Values in Evaluation

Rawls's principle of distributive justice is that social and economic inequalities are to be arranged so that they are of greatest benefit to the least advantaged. This principle is to be given priority over the principles of efficiency and maximization of the good of the greatest number.

The implication is that priority in evaluation should be given to policies that have important redistributive effects, favorable or unfavorable. In the favorable group are policies of maximizing equality of opportunity and distribution of resources. Like the utilitarians, the egalitarians would give priority to income transfer policies. Their aim, however, would be to evaluate not the effectiveness and efficiency of these policies in changing individual behavior but rather their adequacy as devices for income redistribution. The most important question to be asked is, To what extent are these policies successful in reducing income gaps?

Equity of administration of social programs is another priority. The implication here is that evaluation should focus on problems such as the extent to which food stamp programs benefit low-income people rather than the agricultural industries. A major difference between utilitarianism and egalitarianism lies in the priority that each would give to public interest evaluation. In the egalitarian view public interest evaluation should receive equal priority with research on redistribution. The focus should be on threats to equal protection, which are present in the involuntary exposure of sections of the population to risks of physical harm from radiation or other industrial by-products.

Values and Observations

Whereas utilitarians emphasize the construction of standardized measures by which all variables are to be conflated into one dimension, egalitarians emphasize consumer research, observation of social programs, action research to detect inequities, and the construction of multiple indicators of inequality and inequity. Original data collection and experimentation are taken to be less critical than in other approaches. More use is to be made of available data.

There is no perceived need to reduce observations to a single scale; in fact, this is generally thought to be a mistake. The brutal reductionism often entailed in benefit/cost analysis is particularly abhorrent. Naturalistic standards of significance of effect sizes are suspect.

An implication of these assumptions is that evaluation design should not be left wholly to scientists, social or natural. By its very nature, evaluation bridges the humanities and sciences. Interdisciplinary evaluation teams are needed, but in addition, problem areas from different disciplines often need to be brought together in the mind of the individual evaluator.

Significant Effects

The importance attached to equity in social provision by egalitarians leads to a directly opposite view of effect sizes from the one held by utilitarians. To the egalitarians small inequities are important; therefore research should have power to detect them. Accompanying this view is an interest in variance and a critical view of research in which only central tendencies are dealt with. The egalitarian regards the differential or distributive effects of social policies as extremely important. Justice cannot be done on the average. In setting acceptable risks, equal protection of citizens is to be given priority over economic gains to society as a whole.

Type 1 and Type 2 Errors

The egalitarian view of type 1 and type 2 errors is almost the exact opposite of the utilitarian view. Type 2 errors are considered to be more important than type 1 errors; the egalitarian wishes greater assurance of detection of harmful effects or inequities than of the opposite of this; the same is true of benefits of the social services.

Roles of Scientist and Citizen

Of special importance is sensitivity to the point of view of policy "stakeholders" whose interests are often neglected — for example, future generations, noncustomers who are affected by the behavior of corporations that focus only on the needs of customers. Citizen input into policy making and evaluation is a high priority.

THE EGALITARIAN PERSPECTIVE
ON NUCLEAR POWER

In the United States some $100 billion of public funds was spent prior to 1978 in support of the nuclear power industry (Shrader-Frechette, 1980, p. 121). This investment was made in the expectation that nuclear power would supply electricity more efficiently and cleanly than other energy sources. More than a decade of cost-effectiveness research supported these assumptions (Bupp and Derian, 1978, chapter 9).

Recent evaluations of public policy on nuclear power have seriously challenged these assumptions along three main lines: (1) the failure to consider the adequacy of nuclear power compared to other alternatives for replacing petroleum (Lovins and His Critics, 1977); (2) the neglect or concealment of widespread inequities in public policy (Shrader-Frechette, 1980); and (3) invalidity of studies purporting to show favorable benefit/cost ratios (Bupp and Derian, 1978; Bupp, 1979).

Of special interest here are studies focusing on the problem of equity. Shrader-Frechette's recent study (1980) and the work of the Notre Dame group (Sayre, 1977), exemplars in both substance and method, (1) convincingly demonstrate that there are logical flaws in the attempt to evaluate policies by purely descriptive measures without relating these to values and (2) focus sharply on corporate persons as principal actors in evaluation. These contributions are important to evaluations, both of social service policies and policies designed to control hazards.

Logical Flaws in Value-free Outcome Measures

We have already pointed out in Chapter 2 that value-free outcome measures tend to be impoverished. The egalitarians have documented this limitation in detail. Shrader-Frechette's (1980) critical analysis of the logic of the Bethe (1976) and Rasmussen reports (U.S. Nuclear Regulatory Commission, 1975) on this subject are instructive. A major issue addressed in these studies is that of the acceptability of a risk of a major accident resulting from a core melt in a reactor. Both studies affirm that the risk is worth taking. In support of this position, they offer three arguments; the first one is based on the probability of a core melt, the second on comparison with other risks accepted by society, and the third on comparison with natural levels of risk.

Probability of a Core Melt. This probability, which researchers put at 5 $\times$ 10^{-5} per reactor per year is so small, in their view, that the risk is worth taking. Shrader-Frechette attacks this reasoning as an example of the naturalistic fallacy. Her analysis shows that an implicit premise in the Bethe-Rasmussen argument is that all risks of catastrophic consequences in an otherwise benign technology, which have a very low probability of occurring, should be accepted. But it can easily be shown that this premise is invalid for many kinds of risks. Subjecting all persons to chest X rays to guard against tuberculosis is an example. Therefore, probabilities of catastrophe cannot be defined as acceptable merely because they are low.

Some independent justification is required. To base one's conclusion purely on the magnitude of risk is to ignore other critical considerations. First, the people who bear the risk of a core melt may not be those who would benefit from nuclear power. Second, one must inquire into the morality of the risk in view of the legislation in force that limits compensation to 3 percent of property losses. Consequently, persons living near a nuclear plant are deprived of Fifth- and Fourteenth-amendment guarantees of protection of property. Finally, the Bethe-Rasmussen argument assumes that the current level of usage of electricity must be increased; other research shows that this assumption is questionable. There is also reason to doubt the close connection between gross national product and per capita energy consumption assumed by Bethe-Rasmussen.

Comparison with Other Risks Accepted by Society. If a risk is less than or equal to risks that society has accepted in other areas, Bethe and Rasmussen argue that it should be accepted. Thus the expected deaths from a core melt would be much smaller numerically than the number of people killed in automobile accidents.

A flaw in this argument is that society's acceptance of risks is not adequate evidence of the moral acceptability of these risks. Finding the risk of deaths from automobile accidents to be morally acceptable does not make radiation risk acceptable merely because of its magnitude; other considerations are involved. In particular, one must take account of the degree to which risk taking is voluntary.

Comparison with Natural Levels of Risk.   The third argument of Bethe-Rasmussen is as follows: Since the expected increase in cancer deaths due to a core melt is statistically small compared to the base rate of cancer, it ought to be accepted. Shrader-Frechette, however, argues that (1) the persons who are at risk are not the persons who benefit from nuclear power, (2) that to expose a part of the population to an involuntary risk of death for the sake of economic gain for other groups of persons is morally reprehensible, regardless of the numbers involved, (3) that to take the current rate of cancer deaths as the standard for what is moral implies that this rate is acceptable; and (4) that the status quo is accepted as morally desirable. But this argument again rests on the naturalistic fallacy.

Import

Shrader-Frechette's study contributes to our understanding of policy evaluation by its insistence on teasing out the implicit value assumptions in purported value-free analyses. This approach underlines the need to develop an inclusive scheme of values during the planning stage of policy evaluations — a theme that we pursue further in Chapter 4.

Problems in Benefit/Cost Analysis

A further challenge to the effort to develop value-free outcome measures is MacIntyre's analysis of benefit/cost research in the electric power industry (MacIntyre, 1977). He points out that this research requires the identification of an exhaustive set of alternative policies. It may be possible to find the set of all practical alternatives at a particular time. Over time, however, the alternatives change. As alternatives change, so do benefit/cost ratios. This restricts the utility of the method to short-term problems. But evaluation of energy policies must take into account a relatively long time span. This problem arises in any area in which lengthy time periods are involved.

To carry out a benefit/cost analysis one must assume that the benefit of different policies is commensurable, but there is frequently no unique commensurable scale. An example would be the efforts to place a value on the risk of deaths from skin cancer resulting from changes in the ozone layer produced by Concorde jet planes. Cancer risk also occurs from various sources of low-level radiation and from exposure to hazards of many different kinds. To evaluate this risk, one must place a dollar value on a human life. However, this has been done in at least four different ways, none of which has been shown clearly the best. Use of one rather than another of these methods will change the outcome of a benefit/cost analysis. Thus there is no solution that does not depend on arbitrary decisions made by the evaluator. As often as not, such decisions will be a reflection of the evaluator's personal value system.

Use of benefit/cost analysis further presupposes a decision as to whose values will be considered in the analysis. If the analysis is being carried out on behalf of a corporate actor, this choice generally reflects an interpretation of the corporation's mandate. Almost inevitably such interpretations favor some groups of corporate customers over others. Corporations generally interpret their mandate as the satisfaction of wants as expressed in willingness to pay. Wants are taken as sufficient indicators of need. It is not within the corporation's mandate to make any assessment of the nature of the wants or of the consequences of applying them.

In a similar way, the manner in which the corporate mandate is defined is a major determinant of the time scale that will be found to be appropriate for benefit/cost calculations. The mandate is generally defined in terms of present and future customers, but not future noncustomers who may be indirectly affected by the corporation's activities. Thus, problems of disposal of nuclear waste, which have a very long time scale, are easily separated from the needs of present and future customers. Consequently, they are excluded from benefit/cost calculations — a reflection of both the difficulty of defining the group whose interests may be affected and also the preference for relatively short time frames in benefit/cost calculations. Such judgments, often made implicitly, have a major impact on the results.

Focus on Corporate Persons

The scientific and methodological approaches, being concerned with effectiveness, focus more often on persons than on systems or milieu. A survey of forty years of social problems research by Gregg and Associates (1979) shows that this focus on individuals is characteristic of American social research. As noted earlier, the change consultation approach likewise tends to assume that evaluation participants are natural persons.

In contrast, the egalitarians focus on the behavior of large organizations, as illustrated by MacIntyre's analysis cited earlier and also by McKim's study of the practices of the Nuclear Regulatory Commission (McKim, 1977) in evaluating the social aspects of the construction of nuclear power plants. An important part of both studies is the assessment of the need for additional electric power. McKim shows that in practice the determination of needs is restricted to the determination of future demand. The possibility of harmful effects of increased power production is excluded from the analyses, a factor applicable both to nuclear and fossil plant construction. A companion paper by Maher (1977) analyzes the cultural influences that encourage the growth ethic and the concomitant reinforcement by some features of the power industry itself.

INEQUALITY IN THE SOCIAL SERVICES

In evaluating the social services, egalitarians have also challenged the preoccupation with maximizing average effects, exposed logical flaws in efforts to reduce outcome measures to descriptive indices, and brought the behavior of corporate actors into sharp focus.

Variation in Effects

Taking declared policy missions for granted leads to evaluation of the comparative average effects of different policy options. In the egalitarian studies, the announced policy mission is not taken as read; rather, it is viewed as itself a problem for evaluation. A starting point for such inquiry is social stratification research; here, evidence is found of inequalities in life chances (Gil, 1976). The evaluation question can then be formulated as follows: Whatever the declared mission of a social policy, what are its actual distributional effects? These effects are analyzed over the familiar social class categories: income, education, and ethnicity (Neave, 1970; Jenkins, 1974; Gil, 1976; Rein, Nutt, and Weiss, 1974; Gruber, 1980). These studies raise far-reaching questions about the relationship of the social service policies to social stratification; as yet these have not been fully answered. Gruber's research on institutionalization of children and adults is a useful illustration.

Working from census data, Gruber has shown that blacks and whites tend to be institutionalized in different systems. For example, blacks are about five times as likely to be sent to correctional institutions as whites; in particular, black juveniles before the court are about four times as likely to be sent to correctional institutions as whites. Institutionalized whites are more likely than blacks to be found in institutions for the aged and homes and schools for the mentally handicapped. Given that the treatment in correctional institutions is harsher and less rehabilitative than in treatment institutions, blacks are clearly less favored by institutionalization than whites (Gruber, 1980, p. 63).

Reduction of Outcomes to Descriptive Indices

The significance of Gruber's work for policy evaluation lies in the questions it raises about the prevailing practice of reducing outcomes to value-neutral descriptive indices. These questions arise out of efforts to explain the unequal distribution. One explanation is that there is a "good fit" between client and institution. Blacks and whites have different problems and needs. This explanation presupposes that social service professionals are able to make valid assessments of these needs. These are objective, descriptive, and free of the effects of the assessor's personal values. A substantial body of research suggests that this presupposition is untrustworthy — that is, that the assessments are biased by personal, class, and ethnic factors and by the organizational position of the judge (Briar, 1963). Evidence is also substantial that the problems and needs of children in various types of institutions are not much different (Shyne, 1973). No plausible explanations of the variations in institutional placements other than social class and ethnic factors have been found.

The Downward Drift Hypothesis

To explain the problematic data on institutionalization, Gruber focuses on the behavior of organizations rather than clientele. In brief, his argument is that organizational gatekeepers categorize prospective clients in ways that serve the organizations. Desirable clients are those with a capacity to bring to the organization rewards in the form of public approval and financial support. Agencies with discretionary power at the point of admission select the most desirable clients and pass the others along to agencies with less discretionary power — notably correctional agencies.

Import

Gruber's hypothesis has not yet been fully tested. Yet his and related studies raise serious questions about the equitableness of social services. At the very least these studies underline the need for further efforts at policy evaluation inspired by notions of social justice.

THE EGALITARIAN APPROACH: A CRITIQUE

The egalitarian approach fills some serious gaps in the other approaches. It is the only approach that deals with the problem of valuation in an ideal context. Another important contribution is its use of systematic ethical analysis. Policies are probed for implicit ethical models. Drawing on centuries of critical thought, the models are then critically examined. The problem of evaluation is tackled head-on, not converted into a problem of science, of method, or of consultation. Consequently, the egalitarian approach promises to develop evaluation as a field of inquiry in its own right. No separation is needed between evaluation problems approriate for natural and social scientists. These have the same structure.

As it has developed so far, the egalitarian approach suffers from several limitations. At several points it calls into question prevalent policies for dealing with uncertainty. The use of conventional rules of significance, for example, is shown to be a form of naturalistic fallacy. This underlines what is already obvious: that statistical inference theory is not self-contained but depends on an input of independently derived values. The egalitarians have helped to show the seriousness of the error of using naturalistic criteria. As yet, though, there has been no thoroughgoing attempt to develop policies dealing with uncertainty, and a serious gap remains. As Gold put the problem some years ago: To confuse statistical significance with policy significance is known to be a sin; but apart from exhortations to avoid sin, not much good advice is available (Gold, 1969). (This problem is pursued further in Chapter 5 and in Part II of this book.)

A second area of criticism of egalitarian evaluation is that its prescription for greater attention to ethical questions and, in particular, equity is not clearly linked with data collection procedures. Before this problem can be dealt with, a more systematic typology of values must be worked out. Then, a method of connecting values and observations must be shown. Finally, it must be more clearly shown how values are used to pattern experimental observations.

4 A FRAMEWORK FOR VALUATION

EVALUATION AS A FORM OF SOCIAL INQUIRY

We have observed a widespread tendency to assimilate evaluation to whatever discipline the evaluators happen to be prepared in. This is hardly surprising since it echoes a familiar assumption that the world must be put together in the way a university is put together. Nevertheless, it seems apparent that evaluation problems cross the boundaries of the sciences and the humanities. On the one hand, the empiricist's demand for experimental rigor is hard to argue against; on the other, our review of the scientific, methodological, and social change approaches shows that none of these furnishes an adequate basis for valuation. This can be found only in normative concepts and theories, which are not justifiable by facts alone.

Excluding values from evaluation turns out to be self-defeating. Although intended to protect the validity and objectivity of findings, excluding values often diminishes these qualities and may even destroy them. The critical reviews cited in the previous chapters of public policy making on nuclear power, workers' compensation, income maintenance, and inequality in the social services support this contention.

Efforts to reduce problems of valuation to problems of observation and description have, by and large, been unsuccessful. To construct value scales

53

that stand up to empirical tests of reliability and validity, however, does seem feasible (see Chapter 5). Empiricism need not entail a radical reduction of scope.

A reasonably comprehensive framework for valuation may help to avoid the confusion of values with wants, place the obsession with effectiveness in perspective, and sensitize participants to the inequalities in power and influence that are inherent in most evaluation projects. Values that collide should be identified so that priorities can be established. The exclusive policy obscures rather than eliminates this problem.

Evaluation of social policies can be defined as the empirical assessment of the inclusiveness of coverage, adequacy, equitableness, appropriate citizen involvement, and effectiveness of policy formulation, implementation, and outcomes. This definition assumes (1) that the assessment can be guided by observations collected by the procedures of empirical science, (2) that value assessments are not the same as personal preferences and can, when the context is properly specified, be grounded in observational data, and (3) that the values listed in the definition are essential but not exclusive of others that might be relevant in particular cases.

It is also assumed that evaluation as a form of inquiry is a blend of the humanities and sciences and is distinguishable from the many disciplines from which it arose. Evaluation should contribute to policy making but not as a mere technical tool. Evaluators need not be actors on the policy-making stage; most should be observers, critics, and contributors of information. Least of all should they be anxious attendants on the policy-making process, hoping to find ways to be useful.

CONTEXT AND SCOPE OF VALUATION

The following are definitions and examples of the values needed for comprehensive valuation:

1. *Inclusiveness*: the extent to which the policy as implemented reaches the appropriate populations. Thus, workers' compensation policies should cover all workers at risk; or policies meant to deal with the problem of alcoholism should not ignore the needs of any groups of persons at risk.

2. *Adequacy*: the degree to which the policy accomplishes its qualitative goals. Examples of such goals are the reduction of the proportion of the population living below the poverty line, increased employment of handicapped persons, reduction of recidivism rates among released prisoners, protection of the environment, compensation of workers for job-related injuries, or improved safety conditions in coal mines. Adequacy takes into account the total population at risk. It is not restricted to persons who make use of particular services.

3. *Equitableness*: equal distribution of benefits and risks among different groups of persons affected by the policy, or, equivalently, the degree to which the policy is free of systematic disadvantage for ethnic or other groups. Thus, native Indian families should not be subject by a foster care program to more frequent coercion and legal sanctions than other families dealt with.

4. *Effectiveness*: the degree to which persons directly served by the program are benefited in accordance with policy goals. The term *impact* is often employed with a very similar meaning. Effectiveness combined with economy is defined as efficiency or cost-effectiveness. Very often effectiveness itself is measured in economic terms. Adequacy may be thought of as the sum of effectiveness and inclusiveness.

5. *Democratic involvement*: the degree to which the public, persons served, or residents of the areas in which the policy is in effect are enabled to contribute in the planning, implementation, improvement, or termination of the program. In neighborhood service centers democratic involvement is an explicit policy objective, but it is also important to public policies in general. Consider for example, the need for consumer views in evaluating health care, education, and industrial safety regulations. As problems of health hazards to populations from industrial applications become more widespread, the need for involving the public in many different kinds of industrial planning becomes more urgent.

The following are some examples of values applied to specific policies:

1. *Effectiveness of preventive family counseling.* In child care agencies family counseling is used extensively as a means of reducing the incidence of admission of children to care. The counseling is aimed at helping the families cope with the problems that precipitate the need for care. In the case of children who are admitted to care, an effort is made to continue to work with the family to prepare for and hasten the return of children to their own homes. Although foster care agencies all agree about the necessity of close work with the family, uncertainty exists among them as to the most effective ways to offer this service. Questions arise as to the effectiveness of different methods of counseling in reducing the need for care (ADP, 1969). An evaluation may be designed to assess the relative effectiveness of two or more approaches.

2. *Equitableness of foster care admissions.* Foster care placement of children can be traumatic for both the children and the parents. To minimize this trauma, prior planning and preparation with the family are important.

Differences in the frequency with which adequate prior planning is received among different ethnic groups constitute evidence of inequity in the foster care program. Neave (1970) found that native Indian families in British Columbia were only about one-half as likely to have an opportunity for careful planning of the foster care placement as other groups. Northup (1969) found that native Indian children, compared with other groups, tended to remain longer in foster care and to have more moves from one foster home to another while in care; furthermore, they were more likely to lose touch with their families.

3. *Equitableness of occupational safety standards.* Workers in vinyl chloride production plants are at risk of developing several liver diseases, including a rare form of cancer, from inhalation of particles of this substance. There is a lack of definitive evidence as to the levels of hazardous exposure and the cumulative effects of long-term exposure. Governmental health and safety regulatory agencies must select the tolerable level of exposure to vinyl chloride and then enforce standards of protection. A problem in social evaluation is to assess the effectiveness and/or equity of the regulatory procedures (Brown, 1979).

4. *Equitableness of government regulation of toxic waste disposal.* A more complicated regulatory problem is the decision whether to approve a mining company's plan to dump radioactive tailings from a molybdenum mine into an ocean sound that serves as fishing grounds for an Indian tribe and for sports fishermen. A dispute arises as to the possible effects of the dumping on fish stocks; the company maintains that there is no real danger, but local residents cite instances in which similar reassurances by this company proved to be false.

5. *Adequacy of corrections measures.* Gun control legislation is passed by a state legislature with the aim of reducing the rate of violent offenses in which guns are employed. A public policy issue develops around the adequacy of the legislation as a means of dealing with this problem. Representatives of the National Rifle Association argue that the offenses with which the legislation are concerned are committed by professional criminals who will always find ways to obtain guns. Proponents of the legislation point out that in a significant proportion of such crimes the use of the weapon was not planned in advance; therefore, they argue, decreasing the availability of weapons will reduce the frequency of these offenses. A problem of social evaluation is to assess the effects of the gun control legislation on the rate of crimes of violence involving guns in a sample of urban communities (Zimring, 1975).

Contexts of Valuation

Personal Contexts. The personal values of all participants must to some extent influence each step in evaluation. Control over these influences can be only a matter of degree. The use of standardized patterns of observation (see Chapter 7), coupled with the extensive use of peer reviews of studies, serves as main control over personal values in the observational phase of the inquiry. The use of judges in value scaling in such a way as to ensure that the context is not one of purely personal preferences is best considered in the context of the selection of judges, to be discussed later in this chapter.

Standard Contexts. These are less often needed and, compared with personal preferences, are more easily kept from influencing the evaluation.

Ideal Contexts. In selecting the guiding values and in using them in the construction of indices, the relevant context is what is best for society as a whole, in the long run (Kaplan, 1964). We assume that inclusiveness, equitableness, adequacy, effectiveness, and democratic involvement are essential properties of "good" social policies — that, in particular, they should be characteristic of policies governing the social services and regulation of hazards to human well-being.

Characterizing Value Judgments. The context of value scaling is that of characterizing judgments (Nagel, 1961, pp. 492–93). The judges are provided with definitions of the values, trained in their application, instructed in certain limiting rules, and required to map selected points on indices onto values scales (see Chapter 5).

Sources of Values

Values are derived from science and from normative social theories. Scientific values serve as a guide to the observational phase of evaluation; concepts of social justice guide the planning and interpretative aspects. As argued below, this guidance should not be subliminal, but rather should be made as explicit as possible.

RELATING VALUATIONS TO OBSERVATIONS

A distinction must be made between the use of data as grounds for values and as grounds for valuation. The first is an effort to find empirical support for values, and the second an effort to decide on the extent to which some value (e.g., a requirement of equity in distribution of risks) is satisfied by a given state of affairs. It is the latter meaning that is of interest in this study; the former use is discussed only in the context of the problem of the naturalistic fallacy — the attempt to derive "ought" statements from factual statements.

Even armchair valuations may be said to be grounded in data, although the data may be secondhand or casually obtained. Valuation that aims to be comprehensive must look for more solid grounds. A number of problems must be dealt with, some of which are of secondary importance in this study since they have been extensively treated in many other recent works.

Observations That Permit Satisfactory Estimates

The observations must be patterned so as to permit satisfactory estimates. A worker in a vinyl chloride factory might develop cancer of the liver for reasons other than exposure to vinyl chloride; similarly, families receiving different forms of counseling might respond differently for reasons that have nothing to do with counseling. Evaluations must be designed to take into account these possibilities. Random assignment to the two different forms of counseling would minimize the chances that the differences observed at the end of the experiment were the result of differences in the families themselves rather than in the treatments they received. This device is one of several used to make planned rather than haphazard observations; the purpose of this planning is to reduce the risk of misinterpretations of findings.

Stimulated by the classic work on experimental and quasi-experimental designs of Campbell and Stanley (1963), an immense literature concerned with the problem of patterning observations has developed. Cronbach and Associates (1980, pp. 289–313) have recently challenged the conventional wisdom that random assignment to experimental and control groups is always optimal. We attempt to capitalize on this contribution but with no ambitions to contribute substantially to this line of work.

Devices for Data Collection and Measurement

Extensive treatments of the design of observation schedules, structured disguised tests, and other devices for data collection and measurement can be found in the following sources: Kaplan (1964), Nunally (1967), Phillips (1976), Rowe (1977), and Haynes and Wilson (1979). Although evaluators can readily borrow most of what they require on measurement technology from sources such as these, information on the effects of random measurement errors on the outcomes of statistical tests employed in evaluations is harder to find. Basics of this topic are therefore treated in Chapter 6.

One issue needs to be laid to rest: the relative merits of qualitative and quantitative data collection strategies. Taking sides on this issue seems unnecessary, for the decision to employ one or the other of these tactics should be determined by the problem, not the evaluator's methodological preferences. The tactics of qualitative knowing are diverse; they include, for example, introspection, textual and concept analysis, participant observation, and interviewing (Patton, 1980). In its early stages, the development of quantitative measures requires the use of each of these qualitative tactics.

Selection of a point at which to begin this instrument development process is mainly a function of the current state of measurement of a construct and the adequacy of existing measures of the values that are to guide one's project. This implies that qualitative and quantitative measurement are interrelated, not mutually exclusive. Qualitative knowing in evaluation is essentially an articulation of the connections of observations and values. Thus Neave (1970) arrived at "equity" as the orienting value construct for his evaluation of foster care from preliminary analyses of data from agency reporting forms, in conjunction with exploratory interviews with child welfare professionals and with persons served. The data from the reporting forms suggested that a suspiciously large proportion of children in native Indian families were being apprehended by the agency with little prior opportunity for consultation with the parents; the interviews confirmed that there were special difficulties in planning with native families. The consequence of these problems was a series of inequities — native Indian parents not only had little input into admission planning but also were severely disadvantaged at later stages of foster care planning and were more likely than other families to lose touch with the agency and their children. Once aware of the relevance to his work of the construct of equity, Neave was able to develop a measurement index focused on this construct.

The spelling out of meanings from which outcome measures are to be constructed requires consultation with as large a sample as possible of "stakeholders" in the evaluation, particularly intended beneficiaries of a policy and persons likely to be indirectly affected. When fully developed, most measurement devices for use in evaluations yield quantitative data, simply because such data are more precise. Of critical importance in the evaluation problems dealt with in this study are estimates of quantitative relationships of pairs of values, such as exposure to vinyl chloride and the probability of contracting one or more liver diseases, type of correctional regime and probability of recidivism, safety inspection practices, and rate of accident claims. What is at stake in all of these cases is the magnitude of the relationship. In most of the examples we shall employ, the existence of data appropriate for using such measures of relationship will simply be assumed, with few digressions into technology of instrumentation.

Mappings of Measures onto Values

The mappings of measures onto values by setting up rules of correspondence clearly have a decisive effect on the outcome of the evaluation. These rules should be, as fully as possible, justified and made explicit enough to be used by different groups of evaluators. In social research and evaluation texts a sharp distinction is seldom made between outcome scores and value assessments. As a consequence, the drawing of evaluative conclusions is more haphazard than it need be. Over the last twenty-five years, methodology has been developed in the fields of psychophysical scaling and political science and can be used to standardize the process of mapping descriptive indices onto value scales. This utilization can increase the information yield and the comparability of evaluations (see Chapter 5).

Definitions of Significant Results

As noted earlier in Chapter 2, a variety of technical rules of thumb have been employed to define significant differences, gains, or departures from hypotheses. A serious weakness of these devices is their arbitrariness. The use of value scaling permits a nonarbitrary definition: a significant result (e.g., difference) is one for which the corresponding position of the value scale is greater than zero. This value determines the hypotheses to be tested (see Chapters 6–10). Value scales must usually be judgment scales. The crucial step of selecting judges is taken up as a part of the problem of defining scientists' and citizens' roles in evaluation.

COMPREHENSIVE EVALUATION

As pointed out in the Introduction of this text, comprehensive policy evaluation involves taking up fifteen classes of questions, arrived at by cross-classifying the five guiding values with the three evaluation foci of policy formation, implementation, and outcome. Here the fifteen types of questions are described.

Policy Formulation Questions

These questions may refer either to the process or the end result of policy formulation. There are five types of policy questions, the first two referring to the product — the policy as formulated in legislation, directives, or agreements — and the remaining three to the process by which this policy was arrived at.

1. *Need assessment questions.* How complete and adequate was the research on which the need for the policy was determined? Answering this question involves critical review of the planning research that was used at the formation stage. The following specific questions arise: What research was conducted to determine the incidence and prevalence of the problems or needs with which the policy is concerned? Were populations at need or risk clearly identified? How adequate were the means used to project needs over time? What reviews of the research were done? How independent and credible were the reviews? How has the research stood up to criticism?

2. *Impact model questions.* These questions also hinge on reviews of the research that guided the formulation of policy. The "impact model" refers to the assumptions and/or theory of how the policy is expected to work — that is, to satisfy the projected needs or bring about desired changes. At a minimum, three kinds of relationships must be distinguished in the model. First, there must be an abstract formulation of the presumed relationships, such as the economic proposition underlying the Mallar and Thornton (1978) research: recidivism will be reduced by increasing its costs.

Second, there must be a statement of how this general proposition is to be given a particular realization in the policy as implemented — for example, providing financial assistance to newly released prisoners. In another program, the decision might be to achieve this end by increasing the penalties associated with recidivism. Third, the conditions under which the second relationship holds must be set forth — for instance, the minimum length of time payments to prisoners will be needed.

As Aaron points out, social programs are often based on simple faiths that fail to stand the test of experience (Aaron, 1978, pp. 66–71). This observation also seems applicable to energy policies and policies to control industrial hazards. The main questions about the impact model concern its clarity, the adequacy of prior testing of the model, and the degree to which monitoring of unintended effects was provided for. Of critical importance, as well, is the problem of the anticipated difficulty of turning the policy around or slowing it down if it turns out to have unwanted consequences. Collingridge (1980) provides excellent examples as well as a classification of factors that render policy changes difficult.

3. *Questions concerning the source and mechanisms of influence on policy formulation.* How was the policy originated? By whom was it supported and opposed? Whose interests appear to be represented in the policy? Whose, if anyone's, interests are opposed to the policy? By what means was influence brought to bear to create the policy? How were conflicts, if any, resolved? On what basis?

4. *Questions concerning the accessibility of policy formation to influence by citizens.* To what extent was policy making open to influence by the public? Were key decisions made in secret, only to be revealed years later? What mechanisms of public input into the process were used?

5. *Policy enactment questions.* Questions of this type refer to the difference, if any, between the policy as proposed for enactment by legislative or executive bodies and the policy actually enacted. What changes were made? Of what scope? To what effect?

Policy Implementation Questions

1. *Questions concerning the overall inclusiveness of coverage of the policy as implemented.* These questions are more likely than policy formulation questions to require substantially more than library and documentary research. Is there evidence that the policy as implemented covers everyone for whom it is intended? For example, if public policy calls for reliance on private medical insurance, who is effectively covered and who is without coverage of any kind? What are the obstacles to coverage? What alternatives have been found by those not covered? How satisfactory are these?

2. *Compliance of the policy implementation with the qualitative standards initially set forth.* For example, are permissible levels of exposure of the public to radiation adhered to? How adequate is the monitoring? Is it credible? (That is, is it carried out by the power utilities themselves, to whom it is a cost, or by independent monitors?) How accessible is information concerning compliance? How complete is it? How often is it updated?

3. *Questions concerning variance in service quality or protection from hazards received by ethnic, social class, age, or other groups.* Neave's study of inequities in planning of foster placements belongs in this category, as well as Gruber's research on institutional care and studies of the equitable distribution of benefits and risks of technologies.

4. *Questions concerning citizen involvement in policy implementation.* To what degree are citizens involved in program monitoring and planning for continuation, expansion, or termination?

5. *Resource output questions.* Compared to what was initially proposed for enactment, and enacted, what resources have been put into policy implementation? How have these been distributed across various program components?

Policy Outcome Questions

1. *Questions concerning the overall variance in outcomes of the policy as implemented.* This variance is usually across persons, communities, or organizations. Variance over persons is illustrated by Bergin's extensive studies of the variance in outcomes of psychotherapy, in which he concludes that it is a potent force for deterioration as well as improvement (Bergin and Strupp, 1973, p. 19). The significance of studies of overall variance is that they offer evidence as to the need for further inquiry into the question of who is less well served and possible explanations.

2. *Questions concerning adequacy of policy outcomes.* These studies attempt to ascertain the overall impact of policies in comparison with policy aims. Time series studies of the effects of police "crackdowns" on drinking drivers are one example (Campbell, 1972).

3. *Variance in outcomes across ethnic, class, or other groupings.* This category extends the questions about overall variance to a search for inequities in policy outcomes along the lines on which these often occur. Northup's study of the unfavorable outcomes of foster care for native Indian children illustrates this type of question (Northup, 1969).

4. *Questions concerning citizens' roles in monitoring outcomes.* These questions parallel the questions concerning citizen involvement in program implementation. Key questions are, How accessible is information on outcomes? How are these monitored? By whom? With what credibility? How public is the process?

5. *Effects on program clientele.* These questions refer not to whole populations of concern but to persons (organizations or communities) directly served by the program. What are the results for these groups?

The relationship of these fifteen types of questions to evaluation focus and valuation categories is shown in Table 4.1.

Table 4.1. Comprehensive Evaluation: Types of Evaluation Questions by Valuation Categories and Evaluation Foci

Valuation Category	Evaluation Foci		
	Policy Formulation	Policy Implementation	Policy Outcomes
Inclusiveness	Adequacy of need assessment	Overall inclusiveness of coverage	Overall variance in outcomes
Adequacy	Adequacy of impact model	Compliance with standards of implementation	Adequacy of policy outcomes
Equitableness	Sources and mechanisms of influence	Variance in service quality by social class or related factors	Variance of outcomes across social class or other groups
Democratic involvement	Accessibility of policy formulation to citizens	Citizen involvement in policy implementation	Citizen involvement in monitoring outcomes
Effectiveness	Policy enactment	Resource output	Effects on program clientele

APPROPRIATE POLICIES TO GUIDE
UNCERTAIN INFERENCES

Conventionalism versus Specially Designed
Schemes of Inference

Conventionalism in statistical inference is nicely illustrated by an anonymous referee's comment on a paper submitted for publication: "The use of the .05 and .01 levels of statistical significance is a well-established tradition. Because it has common meaning to a large group of scholars, it should not be abandoned merely because of an attack on it by one critic, even though the criticisms are well founded." Opposition to this conventional view has, in fact, been expressed by many critics, among them, Sir Ronald Fisher, one of the inventors of the significance test. Fisher pointed out that the social researcher should never apply a predetermined level of significance to any and all problems in all circumstances; each case, he maintained, must be considered afresh in the light of evidence and current ideas about the problem (Fisher, 1973, p. 45).

An important implication of Fisher's remarks is that, contrary to conventionalist assumptions, the significance test is not a self-contained scheme of inference. As Fisher makes clear by many illustrations drawn from such diverse fields as agriculture, astronomy, genetics, and physics, the choice of null hypotheses and of rejection rules, including the very construction placed on the word "rejection," depends on the norms of evidence that are particular to different fields of inquiry; these norms have little to do with statistics.

Nevertheless, for at least the last thirty years, conventionalism has been the predominant inference paradigm employed in evaluative research. Common practice is to treat the conventional procedure as if it were a packaged computer routine. The researcher need pay little attention to what goes on inside and has only to enter appropriate data into this black box induction machine to obtain a rigorous test of a program effect.

A serious problem with this approach to statistics is the lack of resemblance between the product and what trusting evaluators imagine it to be. In particular, they overestimate the precision and definitiveness of findings, especially negative ones. Grasping the factors that actually determine the outcomes of statistical tests is the only means of avoiding this misunderstanding. More than just the knowledge of the inner workings of the black box is needed. Statistical tests must be carefully designed to suit the requirements of specific evaluation problems. It is a mistake to look on them as a stock of fixed, conveniently precut, rigorous algorithms of inference that can be borrowed at will.

The most serious problem with conventionalism is that it rests on the naturalistic fallacy as discussed in Chapter 2. The conventionalist view must therefore be rejected, and along with it the assumption that the logic of statistical inference is self-contained. We shall assume, on the contrary, that valuation and uncertain inference are interdependent.

On the one hand, all schemes of uncertain inference depend on value judgments — judgments, for example, about what statistical effects are to be considered significant. Conversely, the application of value judgments to data is incomplete without taking into account the random uncertainty of the data. As Fraser (1976) has pointed out, nearly all data in the social sciences are subject to large random errors. But deciding on the degree of random uncertainty to be accepted in an evaluation is a policy issue that can be resolved only by applying value judgments.

Single-School versus Eclectic Approaches

Statistical inference has in recent decades developed along divergent lines, in the process generating many controversies. A number of these are documented in the volume edited by Morrison and Henkel (1970), which sounded a note of doubt concerning the scientific usefulness of generally employed methods of statistical inference.

Barnett (1973, p. 19) sounded a different note, referring with evident relish to the vast range of ideas around which controversy and criticism have developed. Pointing out that not only have many schools developed but that there are appreciable differences of interpretation within each school, Barnett suggests that we resist the temptation to stand up and be counted on one side or another of these conflicts. Rather, we should be thoughtful eclectics, integrating whatever looks most promising as a way of dealing with any particular problem.

One important implication of Barnett's argument is the need for some careful comparative shopping before selecting statistical inference schemes for application to particular problems. No one method of statistical inference is appropriate to all problems in social evaluation. Nor, it should probably be added, is it wise to assume that for any evaluation problem we might have, a fully adequate method of inference exists. Partly as a result of the controversies, there are both a wealth of potentially useful materials and a good deal of room for invention. This task, however, cannot be left entirely to the statisticians themselves since they can hardly be expected to anticipate in detail the needs of social evaluators.

More initiative than just seeking consultation seems to be required. The evaluator must decide on suitable formulations of research questions or hypotheses, then locate the most promising inference approaches. The required judgments are not statistical, but have to do with the fit between evaluation problems and the assumptions of statistical models. For example, evaluators must decide for themselves whether parameters should be treated as fixed or changing, whether credible prior probability distributions are available, and whether it is more useful to control probabilities and let the sizes of confidence intervals vary, or conversely. Only after progressing to this stage can one probably make the most effective use of the guidance of the professional statistician.

The principal themes to be pursued further in this study are connections between values, research design, and inference procedures (Chapters 5-7, 11); relative likelihood analysis as an approach to the problem of assessing plausibilities of hypotheses (Chapters 8, 12); taking account of fluctuating parameters (Chapter 9); and selecting appropriate inference procedures (Chapter 11).

ROLES OF SCIENTIST AND CITIZEN IN VALUATION

Procedural Fairness

Define valuation as the assignment of values to possible findings. To clarify the roles of scientist and citizen in this process it is first necessary to identify the conditions that will maximize fairness. The assumption that potential judges can be sorted into the "biased" and "unbiased" or the "fair" and the "unfair" should be avoided. The multipartisan scientist is probably a mythical creature — no one should be assumed to be unbiased. McGilly (1978) neatly captured this principle in the title of a paper: "My Analysis, Your Ideology, His Bias." Developing an analogy to the principle of imperfect procedural justice is helpful, for it instructs us not to try to assess the justness of each and every conceivable outcome of a judgment process but rather to establish procedures, as in criminal courts, that maximize the likelihood of a just outcome (Rawls, 1972, p. 85). Instead of a general definition of "fairness," I propose the following procedural rules:

1. As argued previously, the task of assigning values to possible effects appears to be inherently judgmental. In practice this means selecting a group of judges to make ratings. (The details of the rating procedure are discussed in Chapter 5.)
2. Inevitably, the judgments are partly intuitive. As Hamblin (1974, p.

112) has suggested, they probably reflect cultural conditioning. Rawls (1972, p. 47) further suggests that in arranging the conditions of judgment we should endeavor not to eliminate intuition but to try to give it free play — that is, to free it from the influence of anxieties and contingencies of personal advantage and disadvantage.

3. It is essential to keep in mind the unequal power relationship of parties to most evaluations, especially the relationships of corporate actors and individuals.

4. Judgments should therefore be independent. To this end, bargaining, intimidation, and appeal to scientific or other authority should be excluded.

5. The selection of priorities among different and possibly conflicting valuations should not be mixed with the task of carrying out the ratings. This would confuse judgments in ideal contexts with characterizing judgments. Therefore, judges should be instructed to rate each of the values independently of the others. For example, judgments of equity should not be influenced by considerations of efficiency, and conversely.

6. In judging the equitableness of policies dealing with protection of human populations from risks, the ratings should be made from the point of view of those who are at greatest risk. For example, since the risks to young children from exposure to low-level radiation are six or seven times what they are to adults, data and ratings of equity should be in reference to children.

7. Both the measure on which ratings were made and the distribution of ratings data should be included in reports. Then an independent team of investigators may repeat the procedure using a different group of judges.

Selection of Judges

The procedural rules are an aid in selecting judges. It is also helpful to take account of two broad types of assessment problems:

Case 1: Risks to Human Well-Being Stemming from Corporate Activity. In this case there is typically a substantial imbalance of power between the corporation and persons at risk. The corporation not only has a greater power to influence the outcome but also a greater freedom to fight the case. Workers whose health is threatened by asbestos, for example, have seldom felt that they were free to risk their jobs. Consequently, they have tended to minimize or ignore the risk rather than fight it (Gersuny, 1981, pp. 68–97).

This inequality at first glance seems to imply that persons actually at risk should not be selected as judges. There may be too great a likelihood that their judgments will be influenced by personal contingent factors. Nevertheless, fairness demands that the ratings be made from the point of view of the victims who are at greatest risk, as suggested earlier. Such a requirement, at least where adults are involved, can be satisfied only by using judges drawn from the risk population (but not involved in a current controversy over a specific risk). They must be trained to keep personal benefits and risks to themselves separate from the valuations. As previous research has demonstrated, such training can be effected by collecting separate ratings of the personal threats (Kogan and Hunt, 1950). Bear in mind that the data on which the ratings are being made consist of points on the index of possible findings, not actual data. This knowledge further helps to minimize the effects of personal factors.

For several reasons scientific specialists on the risk problem should not be selected as judges. First, they are likely to be in the employ, directly or indirectly, of the very corporations whose activities are at issue. Second, their technical competence can be better applied to several related tasks, such as construction of indices of effect, modeling the relationship between exposure and risk or between treatment and outcome, or critical analysis of the research design and of related research. The indices of effects, constructed by measurement specialists, are employed as stimuli for the raters.

Case 2: Valuations of the Effects of Social Services. The role of professionals is the same as that of scientists in risk assessment problems — to help ensure that research procedures are adequate in all respects. Like the scientists, the professionals are interested parties; they have no special claims to competence in valuation. The findings of several studies have suggested that the priorities of social service professionals may be unduly influenced by what is prestigious in the profession; they tend to clash with the priorities of the clients (Crane, Poulos, and Reimer, 1970).

Ruling out professionals, and guided by the principle that the ratings should be made by persons most affected by the service, the judges should be chosen from the client group, a task relegated as part of the planning of service. The research design will often be the service-controlled case study. In other cases, such as studies involving secondary analysis of data from social agency information systems, former clients may be selected.

In some cases the relationship between social agency and clients is, at certain stages, adversarial, as in child neglect and abuse problems and where the professional is an agent of a court. In these situations, favorable conditions for training such judges may not be achievable, and equivalent judges not involved in an adversary role must be employed.

II VALUATION AND OBSERVATION

5 TECHNIQUE OF VALUE SCALING

In social evaluations the hypotheses to be tested against the data must be anchored in the values by which the project is guided. The task of this chapter is to make explicit the relationship between the guiding values and the choice of hypotheses. Since it is natural to formulate the hypotheses in terms of the outcome measures, we first develop a measure of the relationship between values and outcome scores and then show how to use this relationship in formulating hypotheses. One of these, the threshold hypothesis, which asserts that the social intervention being evaluated is of significant value or significantly harmful, plays a crucial role in shaping the evaluation design (see Chapter 7).

We will first discuss several types of value scales, adopting a ratio-level value scale as clearly superior to all other possibilities. This leads to an examination in some detail of the method of *magnitude estimation*, which provides a ratio-level scale of human judgments. Later in the chapter we will learn how to make use of the value scale to identify a threshold hypothesis, as well as additional hypotheses. The chapter concludes with an assessment of the overall usefulness of magnitude estimation in the design of social evaluations.

THE OUTCOME MEASURE AND THE VALUE SCALE

In Chapter 4 it was argued that values serve as the frame of reference not only for the creation of outcome measures but also for the interpretation of the scores produced by these measures. The framework of interpretation is simply a classification of outcome scores into different intervals of the value scale. In evaluating a counseling program, for example, one might attempt to identify a *threshold effects score* marking the dividing line between adequate and inadequate treatment effects. Further discriminations of adequacy can then be made by marking off important intervals of the effects scale on either side of the threshold. A convenient metric would be to make each interval equivalent to one threshold effect. Because these important outcomes, rather than trivial ones, should determine the statement of hypotheses to be tested, and because the statement of the hypotheses shapes the central features of the sampling, data collection, and data analysis designs, it is essential that the units of the value scale be determined at the planning stage.

To create this value scale requires a method of transforming every possible score on the outcome measure into a value category or score. It is helpful to think of this transformation as a mapping — a setting up of correspondences between two measures according to well-defined rules. The resulting value scale could be at a nominal, ordinal, interval, or ratio level of measurement. These different levels of measurement would require different mapping rules. The rule for a nominal-level value scale might be simply to place an outcome score in one of two categories: at least equal to a predetermined threshold level or below this level. Defining the threshold level would be the most difficult step, but any of the following sources of information might be used as points of departure:

1. Results achieved in previous studies using different treatments. At issue would be the degree to which a proposed treatment should improve on the previous ones.
2. Targets set by policy makers — for example, a 15 percent improvement in labor force participation established by a legislative committee as a goal for an employment training program. This goal could reflect projected costs of the program, the expected net aggregate increase in earnings of the trainees who found employment as a result of the program, and projections of the effects of obtaining employment on future labor force participation.
3. The acceptability of progress toward a norm — for example, a 20 percent reduction in the gap in performance on a standardized test of

reading between an educationally disadvantaged group and the population on which the test was standardized.

A group of judges, as described in Chapter 4, should be appointed to review these background data and establish threshold effects. In this kind of task it is important to take the following points into consideration: (1) statistically small effects need not be small in their consequences; (2) the initial effects of treatment may either accumulate or fade over time — if the effects are cumulative, target effects can be kept small, but if the effects tend to fade out, target effects must be large. Evidence on this point should be sought from prior experience and research.

Though nominal value scales are perhaps the most commonly used kind, they often entail a drastic reduction in the range and number of gradations in the outcome measure. This amounts to discarding information.

Rankings

Loss of information could be reduced by equating scores on the outcome measure to ranks on the value scale. Thus, if the outcome measure were expressed in units of exposure to a toxic substance, ranks could be assigned to different degrees of exposure to create a scale of risk. Even though this method would provide more information than nominal mapping, it might still be unsatisfactory because it would indicate nothing about the rate of change in risk as degrees of exposure increased. For setting regulatory standards, information on this point might be essential.

Interval Scales

These scales are marked off in equal units, but no unique origin is determined. A scale of this kind would be a substantial improvement on rankings because it would permit some comparison of the rate of change in the value scale over different intervals of the effect index. The only drawback of this scale would be its lack of an origin.

Ratio Scales

These scales, which define a unique origin, are clearly "best" in discarding no information from the outcome scores. Further, they enable one to determine the changes in the value scale over the full range of the outcome measure *and* the ratios of any two points on the value scale.

The importance of information on rates of change can be made clear by an example. Rainwater (1974) in a study of perceptions of poverty by a sample of householders in the Boston area, analyzed the relationship of ratings of "poorness" to income. He found that the poorness ratings decreased very steeply as annual income for a family of four increased from zero to about $6,000, then began to level off. Therefore, ignoring these changes in slope at different points would have seriously distorted the interpretation of this relationship. Similarly, ratings of the risk of illness associated with an increase of one-third in exposure to low-level radiation might increase much more than one-third, depending in part on the point at which increase in exposure occurred. Such curvilinear relationships are typical in the relationship of outcome scores to values.

Because they permit analysis of these curvilinear relationships where they are present, and also the estimation of zero points, ratio-level value scales are important to social evaluations. We now examine in some detail the *magnitude estimation* method of constructing ratio scales from human judgments.

MAGNITUDE ESTIMATION

The effects scores never speak for themselves, and the process of transforming these scores into a value scale seems to contain an ineluctable element of human judgment (see Chapter 4). The reader may be wondering at this point whether it is at all realistic to expect to quantify human judgments at a ratio level of scaling.

One effective answer is given by the findings of a large volume of research since 1950 in psychophysics, psychology, and political science, in which many ratio scales of human judgments have been created. The psychophysical studies convincingly demonstrate that ratio scales can be obtained of judgments of some twenty physical sensations such as perceptions of brightness or heaviness (Stevens, 1962, 1966). In a series of studies that began about 1960, it has also been shown that the methods used to obtain psychophysical scales can be successfully applied to the scaling of a variety of social attitudes and values (Hamblin, 1974; Shinn, 1969). These ratio scales, while inferior in some important respects to the ratio scales employed in physics (Luce, 1972; Hamblin, 1974), have nonarbitrary zero points and provide information about rates of change in ratings as the stimulus variables increase. As Blalock (1974, p. 5) points out, there is evidence that magnitude estimation is applicable in many different fields.

A hypothetical example from psychophysics (see Stevens, 1956) can be used to illustrate the essentials of this method. Suppose a group of twenty-five observers are instructed to rate the loudness of a series of thirty tones, identical in all respects except decibel level and presented in random order. The experimenter assigns the number 10 to the first tone presented and directs the raters to use this as a standard in estimating the loudness of the subsequent tones. Thus, raters who feel that the second tone was half as loud as the first would assign it a 5. Medians of the twenty-five ratings on each tone are computed and graphed against standard physical measures of the decibel levels. A line is drawn through the resulting thirty points in such a way as to trace their trend as accurately as possible. The line proves to be a curve, rising at a decelerating rate. Graphing the data on logarithmic paper changes the curve to a straight line.

The methods of ordinary linear correlation may be used to measure the fit between the logarithmic measures of decibel level and the median ratings. In a typical experiment, this proves to be about .97, indicating that one can reproduce with a high degree of accuracy the decibel measures from the median ratings. Since the linear regression equation connecting the two sets of scores preserves the ratio properties of the decibel measures, the ratings constitute a ratio scale of loudness. Many examples of successful scaling of human judgments of sensory perceptions have been reported by Stevens and others (for a useful summary of these studies see Stevens, 1966).

Detailed accounts of the methodology of magnitude estimation have been provided by Stevens (1956, 1962, 1966), Hamblin (1966, 1974), and Shinn (1969). We shall briefly outline the main steps and then introduce further details of certain steps in which the reader will need to develop skill to use the method. The main steps are as follows:

1. Select an appropriate group of judges — perhaps a group of residents of a particular locality or employees exposed to an industrial hazard (see Chapter 4). Stevens suggests that from twenty to thirty judges are needed, though Hamblin (1962) and Shinn (1969) obtained excellent results with seventeen to twenty judges. In evaluations around which several groups are in conflict, it may be advisable to obtain separate magnitude estimates from each group (as discussed later in this chapter).
2. Train the judges in magnitude estimation techniques; obtain the magnitude estimates.
3. Calculate the median of each estimate over the group of judges.
4. On ordinary graph paper plot each median estimate against the outcome score on which it was based. Draw a line through the points,

fitting the trend of the points as closely as possible. If the line is approximately straight, extrapolate it to the horizontal axis and proceed to step five. If it is curved, proceed to the exhibit adapted from Hamblin later in this chapter.

5. Determine the point at which the extrapolated line intersects the horizontal axis. If this is not the origin, read off the distance from the origin. Subtract this from each effect index score.

6. Using standard correlation techniques compute the correlation between the adjusted effect scores and the median estimates. Square the correlation coefficient.

7. If the squared correlation coefficient is in the neighborhood of .85 or larger, the mapping of outcome scores onto the values may for most purposes be considered sufficiently accurate. Failure to achieve this means that the training procedures and the line of best fit drawn in step 4 should be reviewed for possible sources of inaccuracy. If there is reason to suspect that the straight line is an unsatisfactory fit to the data, the procedures of finding relative origins, described below, should be tried.

8. Repeat the scaling procedure for each value scale required. In some cases, different groups of judges may be needed for different value assessments.

METHOD OF OBTAINING MAGNITUDE ESTIMATES: EXHIBIT 1

Details of the method of obtaining magnitude estimates are illustrated in the following example. As a project in scaling of evaluative data, four sets of magnitude estimates were obtained from eighteen graduate students in the School of Social Work at the University of British Columbia in 1977. All of the students had experience in family services under public or private auspices. The students were asked to make magnitude estimates based on the following outcome scores: percentage differences between an experimental and control group in the number of families receiving favorable child-care ratings; percentage increase in couples showing decreased scores on marital dissatisfaction measures; percentage of graduates of a youth employment training service who secured jobs within twelve months; percentage reduction in accidents following introduction of an industrial inspection program.

Data Collection Procedures

The following procedures were used to obtain the magnitude estimates. With the exception of step 3, they are taken directly from Hamblin (1966, p. 18). Wording of step 3 varies slightly for each of the four problems.

1. Interview observers individually. Start by teaching them how to estimate magnitudes using numbers. Using an unlined paper with 9 dots printed 1.3, 2, 4, 5.5, 8, 11, 14, and 19 centimeters from the bottom, give the following instruction:

"We'll start by teaching you how to use numbers to measure things. I want you to judge how far these dots are from the bottom of this paper. If this dot (point to the 4 cm dot) is 100 units from the bottom of the paper, how far from the bottom of the paper is this dot? (point to the 8 cm dot) This dot? (point to the 2 cm dot)"

If the observer gives numbers that approximate the appropriate ratios, have him give the distance estimates for the other dots. If the observer gives numbers that are badly out of ratio (for example, a 110 instead of approximately 200 for the 8 cm dot and a 90 instead of around 50 for the 2 cm dot), proceed as follows:

"Is this (8 cm) dot a third as far, half as far, twice as far, three times as far, or four times as far as this (4 cm) dot?" The observer will usually reply, "Twice as far."

"If it is twice as far and this first dot is 100 units from the bottom, then how many units is this second dot from the bottom?". . .

2. Once the distance estimates are completed, plot the data on logarithmic coordinates, with the observer's estimates on the Y-axis and the distances on the X-axis. . . .

3. Ask the interviewee: Imagine a family support and counseling program for families with a history of physical neglect and abuse of their children. The effectiveness of such a program might be judged by the percentage of families obtaining favorable ratings of child care following twelve months of treatment, compared with a control group monitored over the same period. If a program which achieved a 10% difference between groups is given an effectiveness score of 50, how effective would be a program which achieved a 25% difference? 5%? 50%? 15%? 65%? 35%? no difference? (Note: the interviewer randomly varied the order of these percentages for each respondent.)

4. At least once, when you are about half through, check on ratios. . . .If there is any question even, it is better to start again, perhaps after going through the instructions a second time. . . .

5. If additional series of estimates are taken from an observer, let him rest periodically, about 2 minutes for every 10 minutes of estimations. Keep good eye contact, show continued interest, and he will ordinarily respond accordingly. You may give the observer previous estimates when he asks, but usually he will not ask if you sit so he cannot see the numbers you have written down. . . .

6. Usually 30 sets of estimations are desirable; 2 sets from 15 observers or 1 set from 30. Remember, however, it is accuracy and not the amount of data that counts most.

This procedure was repeated, using as examples a marriage counseling program, an industrial safety inspection program, and a youth employment training program.

Findings

A curvilinear relationship between the outcome scores given the respondents as stimuli in step 3 was found in three of the four programs, and a close approximation to a linear relationship in one, the marriage counseling program. In the three curvilinear cases the line of best fit increased at a decelerating rate.

Squared correlations between the logarithms of the outcome measures and of the judgments of effectiveness were child abuse services, .91; marital counseling, .90; youth employment service, .85; and safety inspection program, .92.

FINDING RELATIVE ORIGINS: EXHIBIT 2

The following is adapted from Hamblin (1974, p. 83):

Unfortunately, there are no simple, rigorous algorithms for determining relative origins when testing for power functions, but in mathematical experiments in which I have used magnitude scaling, I have followed several steps which produce reasonably good results.

1. Plot the data on arithmetic coordinates and, using a ruler or a French curve, draw a line approximating a least-squares fit to the data.

2. Extrapolate that line to a relative origin. This is not particularly easy to do with a power function because its curvature increases substantially as the relative origin is approached.

3. On the basis of the extrapolation, estimate the relative origin and use it appropriately in correcting the measurements of the stimulus variable. Next, on logarithmic coordinates, plot the corrected stimulus measurements and, if desired, the uncorrected stimulus measures against the response or attitudinal measures.

4. If the plot of the corrected data approximates a straight line, assume that the estimated origin constant is correct, and that the data may be described by a power function. If the plot still shows a curvature, it is possible that the estimate of the origin is incorrect. Hence, one may wish to attempt a second estimate and

repeat step 3. If subsequent estimates of the relative origin, within what seems to be the allowable range on the arithmetic plot, continue to yield a curvature on the subsequent logarithmic plot, one may assume that a power function does not describe the data under consideration.

MEANING OF THE RELATIVE ORIGIN

The meaning of relative origins is best understood by looking at illustrations. Rainwater (1974), for example, found that a graph of magnitude estimates of "poorness" against annual income for a family of four crossed the horizontal axis at an income level of approximately $10,000, indicating that this was the level below which a family should be considered poor. Similarly, the graph of the median estimates by the social work students (Exhibit 1) of effectiveness as a function of reduction of foster care placements crosses the horizontal line at the 8 percent point, whereas a similar graph based on percentage of couples showing improvement in marital satisfaction crossed the horizontal axis at 14 percent. Evidently, as a result of the urgency of the problem of physical risk to children, the social work students saw an 8 percent gain as evidence of effectiveness but required a larger percentage gain as evidence of effectiveness of marital counseling.

A most important application of relative origins is to mark the point on the outcome measure corresponding to a threshold effect (see Chapter 4). This is a way of arriving at an estimate of a minimally adequate result, which may form the threshold hypothesis to be tested. As shown in Chapter 7, this value is crucial to the evaluation design.

UNDERSTANDING POWER FUNCTIONS
OF OUTCOME SCORES

The accelerating or decelerating curves referred to in the examples of magnitude estimates can be described by equations of the form:

$$\text{value scale score} = c\,(\text{outcome score})^n, \tag{5.1}$$

where c is a constant that is estimated from the data by standard regression methods and n is the power to which the outcome score must be raised to equal the corresponding score on the value scale.

If n is less than 1, the graph of the relationship ascends rapidly at first, then decelerates; it is concave downward. If n is greater than 1, the curve rises at an accelerating rate; it is concave upward.

Plotting the data on logarithmic graph paper is equivalent to taking the logarithm of each side of equation (5.1). Applying the elementary rules of logarithms yields:

$$\log (\text{value scale score}) = \log c + n \log (\text{outcome score}). \qquad (5.2)$$

This equation is of the same form as the equation of a straight line used in ordinary linear regression analysis.

BIPOLAR VALUE SCALES

A bipolar scale has zero at the center, with positive values to the right of zero and negative ones to the left. Such scales are frequently important in evaluations, if only to allow for the plausibility of negative results. The work of Ekman (1961), Hamblin (1966), Stevens (1966), Shinn (1969), and others has led to the important discovery that power functions of conceptually opposite variables such as satisfaction and dissatisfaction seldom have precisely the same exponents. Therefore, magnitude estimates of the ineffectiveness of a program would not necessarily yield a graph of the same slope or threshold effect as a graph of effectiveness estimates. The general shape of the graph would be similar.

This means that "effectiveness" and "ineffectiveness" should not be estimated together. Instead, the magnitude estimates for each value should be obtained separately, and separate calculations of the relative origins, exponents, and correlations should be carried out. After correcting for relative origins, the two data plots may then be arranged together on the same graph on either side of the origin.

MULTIPLE MEASURES OF EFFECT FOR EACH VALUE SCALE

Magnitude estimates will ordinarily be needed from two or more sets of outcome variables. For example, to collect data that will provide adequate evidence of the effectiveness of a program of preventive family counseling in reducing the risk of foster home placement of children, we might decide to employ as outcome measures three different subscales of the Geismar-Ayres index of family functioning, such as the child-care scale, the health-care scale, and the scale of family cohesiveness (Geismar and Ayres, 1960).

In cases like this, it is necessary to collect magnitude estimates of the combined effects of the several outcome measures on the value scale. After converting the data to logarithms, ordinary multiple regression procedures may be employed to estimate the exponents and the multiple correlation. Detailed examples are given by Shinn (1969), Hamblin (1966, p. 78), and Hamblin (1974, p. 99). There is evidence that at least three outcome measures may be mapped onto a value scale in this way (Hamblin, 1974).

UNITS OF THE VALUE SCALE

The numbers in which the magnitude estimates are expressed are in a sense arbitrary; they are determined by the number given the raters as a reference point or standard. Arithmetical convenience aside, any other number would yield the same results. In consequence of this arbitrary selection of a standard, the units employed in the value scale have no straightforward reference to the real world.

A simple method of calibrating the value scale to make its real-world reference more clear is to mark it off in threshold score units. Then each score is expressed as a fraction, proper or improper, of threshold units. This is a convenient metric, and its relevance to guiding values is clear.

We make use of this scale in two principal ways: (1) to test hypotheses, for example, a hypothesis that the true outcome is in some specified interval of the value scale; (2) to examine the rates of change in the value scale over different intervals of the outcome measure, especially important in cases in which the value scale rises or falls steeply over some intervals. Turning points and intervals over which the value scale levels off are also informative.

MAGNITUDE ESTIMATION AND SOCIAL DISSENSION

Social evaluations, being caught up in historical time and place, can make no claim to the invariance of findings to which social science aspires. One must be conscious of the possibility not only of change in values over time but also of significant differences in valuations among different groups.

The findings and import of most social evaluations in recent years have been vigorously disputed; examples are the debates surrounding Coleman's study of equality of educational opportunity (Coleman, 1966), Headstart (see the review of conflicts around this project in Rossi and Williams, (1972), and some fifteen studies in social work debated by Fischer (1976) and others.

In part, these disputes inevitably result from the comparatively primitive methodology of social evaluation as it has groped toward maturity. But probably more important, they reflect competing interests and value perspectives. Frequently, these differences in interests are played out around methodological issues. In this way values and methodology may become confounded.

In such cases getting hold of magnitude estimates obtained separately from the groups representing the clashing perspectives can serve a useful purpose. Obtaining these separate magnitude estimates in advance of data collection provides a reading that is uncontaminated by study findings on the extent to which there is prior disagreement on valuations among the contending groups. This knowledge may lead to a reconsideration of the feasibility of the study or of the objectives; in any case it will help to clarify what is really at issue. When it is clear that the disagreements center on the import of findings rather than on the methods by which they are to be arrived at, the appropriate political mechanisms can be set in motion to deal with the disputes. Typically, the political mechanism is a public commission or legislative committee, for whom the magnitude estimate data will also be relevant.

MAGNITUDE ESTIMATION AS A TOOL OF SOCIAL EVALUATION

More than most social measurement methods, magnitude estimation is grounded in a body of findings that have stood up under replication. Moreover, the excellence of fit of the data to the power functions used as models is unusual in social science research. For social evaluations, a most important advantage of this accuracy of modeling is that it facilitates the location of threshold effects (i.e., relative origins), which provide the basis for statements of threshold hypotheses.

Although from the beginning there have been methodological criticisms of magnitude estimation (Luce, 1972), these have centered mainly on the meaning, in social science terms, of the findings of magnitude estimation studies. The paper by Krantz (1972), proposing a theory of magnitude estimation, reviews some of the disagreements in this area. There seems to be little dispute about the accuracy of the findings nor about the usefulness of magnitude estimation as a scaling device. Hamblin (1974) provides a summary of criticisms of this method and rebuttals of the criticisms.

An important advantage of magnitude estimation for social evaluations is the availability of a check on the adequacy of the fit of the data to the power function used to summarize the relationship. Provided that data collection procedures have been carefully carried out, a poor fit to the model

Table 5.1.   Applications of Magnitude Estimation

Value Scale	Outcome Measure
Effectiveness	Difference in proportions of "successes" in treatment and control groups
Equity	Odds ratios of unfavorable side effects for different groups
Acceptability of risk	Increased probability of illness (e.g., leukemia) resulting from an industrial hazard
Adequacy	Reduced incidence of automobile thefts

indicates a lack of consensus among the raters as to the relationship between outcome scores and values. An attempt should be made to pinpoint the source of this disagreement before carrying out the evaluation. The problem may lie in an inappropriate choice of outcome measure to represent the value, or in valuation conflicts between members of the group calling for separate estimates from different subgroups. If a good fit to the model cannot be achieved, simpler methods, as outlined in the beginning of this chapter, may be used.

Perhaps the main limitation of magnitude estimation as a tool in social evaluation is its limited experience. The applications in Table 5.1, however, look promising.

6 RELATIONSHIPS THAT DETERMINE OUTCOMES OF TESTS OF HYPOTHESES

A hypothesis test involves the application of a decision rule to an *outcome probability* — that is, a probability that if a specified hypothesis were true, the outcome observed in the data would have occurred. Chapter 5 was devoted mainly to methods of deriving the threshold hypothesis.

In this chapter we examine in detail the relationships that determine the results of a test of the threshold hypothesis. First we define the outcome probability and show how this probability is linked both to the threshold hypothesis and to an alternate hypothesis. Then we show how to substitute a discrepancy measure for the outcome probability — a step that will greatly simplify subsequent calculations. The remainder of Chapter 6 analyzes the direct determinants and then the indirect determinants of the outcome probability to pave the way for planning the details of the research design, which will be taken up in Chapter 7.

THE OUTCOME PROBABILITY

To test an evaluative hypothesis we first devise a measure of the consistency of the hypothesis with the data we have collected. For example, if the threshold hypothesis is that the true difference in the proportions of successful outcomes for two treatments is .00, but we find a difference between samples of .40, we calculate the probability of finding such a large difference *if our hypothesized value of .00 were correct.* This probability — call it the *outcome probability* — measures the consistency of the data with the threshold hypothesis.

In itself, this information would not enable one to decide whether to accept or reject the hypothesis. It would still be necessary to adopt some rule concerning the degree of inconsistency of the hypothesis with the data to be taken as grounds for rejection of the hypothesis. Selection of this rule, which depends primarily on guiding values, is taken up as a part of study design (Chapter 7). A prior problem is to sort out the determinants of the outcome probability. This sorting out is essential to the correct understanding of the effects of one of these determinants — the intervention being evaluated. If this were the only determinant, evaluation would be comparatively simple. In reality there are multiple determinants; some of these, such as sample size, are consequences of plans made by the evaluator.

If we overlook the effects of these factors on the outcome probability, we run the risk of becoming merely the discoverers of our own assumptions. Other things being equal, the greater the research budget, the larger the sample and the greater the probability of rejecting a false hypothesis; thus the findings depend on the budget. To avoid this restriction we must use our heads and not simply the budget to determine sample size.

FORMULATING THE NULL AND THRESHOLD HYPOTHESES

An outcome probability, as just defined, is linked to a hypothesis; different hypotheses have different outcome probabilities. Hypotheses are always tested against alternative hypotheses, which may be formulated in several different ways. Therefore, before we can calculate the outcome probability and sort out its determinants, we must formulate the evaluative hypotheses.

In routine statistical inference we would simply set up a null hypothesis that the effect we were interested in is zero and an alternative hypothesis that it is not zero (or greater than zero). But the most useful alternative hypothesis for social evaluations is the *threshold effect,* as defined in Chapter 5. Therefore, the null and alternative hypotheses should be formulated as follows:

Null hypothesis: the true effect is zero.
Alternative hypothesis: the true effect is at least equal to the *threshold effect.*

The threshold effect is important because it represents, in the case of social programs, the borderline between effects of positive value (greater than zero on the value scale) and of less than positive value; in the case of evaluation of hazards, it represents the point at which there is sufficient risk to health or safety to warrant concern. In either case the threshold effect can be defined as the smallest difference from zero on the outcome measure that we wish to detect with assurance. The degree of the discrimination — the size of the threshold effect — is of major importance in planning an evaluation because of the following principle: the smaller the effect to be detected, the larger must be our sample. This principle is explored a little later in greater detail. In brief, we design our research so that the observed effect must be at least equal to the threshold effect before we will reject the null hypothesis.

The threshold hypothesis is thus pivotal to the research design, but need not be the only hypothesis to be tested. Indeed, to take full advantage of the data, one should, after testing for threshold effects, shift the focus to comparisons of outcome probabilities of a range of hypotheses at intervals on the value scale and arrive at a plausible estimate of true effects (Chatper 8). To arrive at such an estimate, a most effective device is a plot of outcome probabilities against the value scale over its entire range (for an example see Figure 11.1).

Specifying null and threshold hypotheses sets the stage for bringing out the determinants of the outcome probability associated with these hypotheses. These are of two kinds: the direct and the indirect. The indirect determinants act on one or more of the direct determinants rather than directly on the outcome probability.

THE DISCREPANCY MEASURE (D) AS A
PROXY FOR THE OUTCOME PROBABILITY

The discrepancy measure is the difference between the effect observed in the samples and the effect that would be expected in the long run if the null hypothesis were true. Label this measure D. Then D has two properties that make it a convenient proxy for the outcome probability: (1) the larger the value of D, the smaller the outcome probability, and conversely (this is a one-to-one relationship, in that for every value of D there is a unique outcome probability); (2) calculation of D is much simpler than calculation of outcome probability. Therefore, in what follows the former is used as a proxy for the latter. Of course, the calculation of D depends on a choice of a sample statistic and probability model: D thus has a number of different calculation formulas.

Two formulas for D most often employed in social evaluations are based, respectively, on differences between two sample proportions and differences between two sample means. After becoming familiar with the determinants of these versions of D, one can readily extend the analysis to other cases by making use of formulas for D available in sources such as Cohen, (1969), Cleary, Linn, and Walster (1979), and Walster and Cleary (1970).

A formula for D in the case of two proportions is:

$$D(ppns) = \frac{p_1 - p_2}{\sqrt{\dfrac{p_1 q_1}{n_1} + \dfrac{p_2 q_2}{n_2}}},\tag{6.1}$$

in which p_1 and p_2 refer to the two sample proportions; q_1 and q_2 are equal to $(1 - p_1)$ and $(1 - p_2)$, respectively; and n_1 and n_2 are the two sample sizes. The value of p_1 is hypothesized to be greater than that of p_2.

$D(ppns)$ is for reasonably large samples normally distributed with a mean equal to zero and variance of one.

The corresponding discrepancy measure for two sample means is similar in form:

$$D(means) = \frac{\bar{x}_1 - \bar{x}_2}{\sqrt{\dfrac{s_1}{n_1} + \dfrac{s_2}{n_2}}},\tag{6.2}$$

in which $\bar{x}_1$, $\bar{x}_2$, n_1, and n_2 are the respective sample means and sample sizes, and s_1 and s_2 the sample standard deviations. The value $\bar{x}_1$ is hypothesized to be larger than $\bar{x}_2$. Like $D(ppns)$, $D(means)$ is normally distributed.

DIRECT DETERMINANTS OF THE OUTCOME PROBABILITY

The Falsity of the Null Hypothesis

By the null hypothesis, in the case of two sample proportions, $p_1 - p_2 = 0$, as opposed to the threshold hypothesis, which asserts that $p_1 - p_2$ is at least dp. The null hypothesis is, therefore, false to the degree that $p_1 - p_2$ is greater than zero. In other words, the more false the null hypothesis, the greater the value of the numerator on the right-hand side of equation (6.1), and the greater the value of $D(ppns)$; consequently, the smaller the outcome probability. It may easily be seen that this holds for $D(means)$ as well.

Sizes of the Two Samples

Increasing one or both sample sizes decreases the denominator on the right-hand side of equations (6.1) and (6.2), which has the effect of increasing the value of $D(ppns)$ and D(means). Thus the larger the sample sizes, other factors being equal, the larger the value of the discrepancy measure, and the smaller the outcome probability.

The Sample Standard Deviations

The effect of sample standard deviations on the size of the discrepancy measure is most easily seen in equation (6.2), where the standard deviations are represented by s_1 and s_2. Increasing these quantities will increase the denominator on the right, which, in turn, will decrease the value of D(means). This also applies to formula (6.1), inasmuch as the sample variance for proportions is a function of the terms p_1q_1 and p_2q_2. Thus, the greater the sample variances, the smaller the value of the discrepancy measure and the greater the outcome probability.

We now turn to the indirect determinants, which are three in number: (1) measurement errors, (2) inconsistent treatments and (3) the evaluator's selection of type 1 and type 2 error probabilities.

UNRELIABILITY, INVALIDITY, AND SAMPLE VARIANCES

Reliability and validity may respectively be defined as the proportion of "true" variance in the outcome measure and the correlation of the outcome measure with a criterion. Since information on both reliability and validity is not always available, we at first present their effects separately.

Unreliability

Unreliability increases observed variance compared to true variance, as shown in detail by Cleary, Linn, and Walster (1970). Thus, if we designate the true sample variance of one of the samples by $(st)^2$ and the additional variance due to measurement error by $(se)^2$, the observed sample variance will be equal to $(st)^2 + (se)^2$, provided that the measurement errors are random and approximate a normal distribution around a mean of zero. Therefore, the greater the random measurement error, the less the value of

D(means), and the greater the outcome probability. The same argument applies, to a reasonable approximation for large samples, to $D(ppns)$.

Invalidity

As shown by Cleary, Linn, and Walster (1970), the effect of invalidity on the value of D is to decrease it. The value of D, calculated from samples to which only partially valid outcome measures have been applied, can be estimated by the following relationship:

$$D(\text{calculated}) = r \times D(\text{true}), \qquad (6.3)$$

where the respective D's are the calculated and true values, and r is the correlation of the outcome measure with a criterion.

The simultaneous effects of unreliability and validity may be estimated by the equations:

$$D(\text{true}) = \frac{\sqrt{\text{reliability}}}{\text{validity}} \times D(\text{calculated}); \qquad (6.4)$$

$$D(\text{calculated}) = \frac{\text{validity}}{\sqrt{\text{reliability}}} \times D(\text{true}). \qquad (6.5)$$

Thus, if validity is .5 and reliability is .8, the observed value of D will be about $.5/\sqrt{.8} = .56$, or 56 percent of the value we would expect with error-free outcome measures. This underestimation may be reduced by increasing the reliability and validity of the outcome measures, or may be compensated for by increasing the sample size sufficiently to increase the value of D in the same proportion (as discussed in the next section).

EFFECTS OF INCONSISTENT INTERVENTION EFFECTS

An assumption underlying the methods of hypothesis testing just sketched is that the treatments being evaluated are applied consistently to every subject; in the case of exposure to harmful substances, this amounts to assuming that each subject received equal exposure. Such an assumption is rarely satisfied completely and may be seriously in error. Thus social workers or other professionals providing treatments may perform unequally, or workers in the same plant may for a variety of reasons receive different degrees of exposure to a hazard.

A study that provides a convincing demonstration of the need to take into account the variations in the performance of social workers is a master's thesis by W. McGregor (1968; later published in revised form by the ADP, 1969).

The following excerpt from an evaluation of social work services shows the effect of variations in worker performance on outcome scores:

> In order to control for the major input variable, the treatment worker, we examined the relationship between Q-Sort scores and movement (change in family functioning).* The Q-Sort scores, which are the subject of another monograph,** are the correlation coefficients of the relationship between workers' rating or sort and the optimum sort. (The optimum sort describes an "ideal family-oriented worker.") Because some caseloads had more than one caseworker, a problem arose with respect to assigning Q-Sort scores. In two instances, the workers in question were with the project for less than six months. On these cases, their scores were ignored. Caseload number four's original worker, however, was replaced after one year and hence a weighted average was substituted.
>
> *There are discrepancies between Q-Sort cited in this study and the original monograph. This is the result of the correction of an arithmetical error and recomputation of the scores using a more appropriate statistical procedure not available at the time of the original study. Goodman and Kruskal's coefficient of rank association G was used to compute scores cited in this monograph. [footnote to ADP, 1969, p. 69]
>
> **See Area Development Project, Research Monographs II. [Ibid]

Three Q-Sort scores were computed, the first two as a result of the individual ratings of all workers by the Treatment Supervisor and the Project Director, and a third rating representing the mean of the previous two. The results of our analysis indicate that the immediate supervisor of treatment workers is the best predictor of worker effectiveness. Movement was significantly related to Q-Sort scores for the following family functioning categories:

Combined Rating — Project Director & Supervisor

	Correlation	Probability
Social Activities	.3842	.0011
Home and Household Practices	.2728	.0231

Project Director

	Correlation	Probability
Use of Community Resources	− .2353	.0478

Treatment Supervisor

	Correlation	Probability
Social Activities	.4118	.0005
Home and Household Practices	.2909	.0141

To examine the performance of individual workers in greater detail, each caseload was compared separately in terms of movement relative to the total control group. Caseload number two showed significant improvement over control in seven of the eight categories. This ranged downwards to caseload five, where there was only one category significantly different from control. However, in this instance, the correlation was negative. [Excerpt from ADP, 1969, p. 69]

Data like these have a number of implications for the design of social evaluations. First, the problem of variability of treatment needs to be taken into account at the planning stage. Providers of service not only must be well trained but also required to undergo careful monitoring of performance. The monitoring, however, should not be done at the conclusion of the evaluation, as in the McGregor study, but early enough to permit corrective training to be initiated. In studies of risks, safety programs, and the like, data should be collected on individual variations in exposure.

It will not always be possible to estimate the effects on the outcome probability of inconsistencies in intervention effects. A simple model of the effects of such inconsistencies, based on analysis of variance and using widely available computer packages, may sometimes be applied. Thus groups of subjects treated by different social workers can be compared on mean outcome score, and analysis of variance can be used to estimate the increase in the variance of outcome scores attributed to different workers (for a very similar model see Boruch and Gomez, 1979). Sample sizes can then be increased to offset this increase in variance in the treatment sample; if the budget will not permit such an increase, the extent of underestimation of treatment effects can at least be taken into account in interpreting the findings.

The main problem in using this method is establishing that the performance data satisfy the conditions for analysis of variance (Freund, 1971). A transformation of the data may sometimes be found that will satisfy these conditions.

EFFECTS OF PROTECTION AGAINST TYPE 1 AND TYPE 2 ERRORS ON SAMPLE SIZE REQUIREMENTS

Recall these two definitions: type 1 error is the rejection of a true null hypothesis; type 2 error is the acceptance of a false null hypothesis. We have already noted that sample sizes, through their effect on variance estimates, are related to D. They are also related to the probability of type 2 error; moreover, the probability of type 2 error is inversely related both to the probability of type 1 error and to sample size.

These relationships can be stated quantitatively in a number of different ways. A particularly useful form is an equation expressing sample size as a function of protection against type 1 and type 2 errors — that is the probabilities of not committing these errors. To simplify calculations we again use, as a proxy for these error probabilities, their corresponding Z scores on the horizontal axis of the standard normal distribution. We carry out separate calculations for case 1 — difference in two proportions — and case 2 — difference in two means.

Difference in Two Proportions: Case 1

Since sampling errors are unknown at the stage of planning the sample size, $D(ppns)$ cannot be calculated. However, Cohen's h is a convenient, normally distributed discrepancy measure, defined as follows:

$$h = 2 \arcsin \sqrt{p_1} - 2 \arcsin \sqrt{(p_2)}, \qquad (6.6)$$

in which p_1, p_2, and dp have the same meaning as in equation (6.1) and arcsin is the inverse sine function readily available on small electronic calculators or in tables. The main advantage of using the arcsin function is that it ensures that h is normally distributed; additional advantages are pointed out by Cohen (1969, p. 175).

As an example of h, if $p_1 = .40$, $p_2 = .15$, using Cohen's tables (Cohen, 1969, p. 176) we obtain:

$$h = 2 \arcsin \sqrt{.40} - 2 \arcsin \sqrt{.15} = .58.$$

This value of h may be adjusted for the effects of unreliability and validity by multiplying it by the expression: validity/(square root of reliability). Suppose that reliability is .89 and validity .81; then the adjustment is $.81/\sqrt{.89} = .86$. The adjusted value of h is therefore $(.86)(.58) = .49$. If Pearson's r is not applicable to the outcome data, correlation may be measured by use of the correlation ratio (Nunally, 1967). To obtain *required sample size*, substitute the adjusted value of h into the following equation:

$$n = 2 \frac{(Z_{1-a} + Z_{1-b})^2}{h^2}. \qquad (6.7)$$

The Z scores correspond to probabilities, fixed in advance, of *not* committing type 1 and type 2 errors. If, for example, we have decided we want these probabilities to be .95 and .90, we must use a table of the normal curve. We find that these two scores are 1.65 and 1.28. Substituting these values into equation (6.7), together with the adjusted value of .28 obtained for h, gives a sample requirement of 219. Each sample must be of this size. In this case it might be more economical to first try to increase reliability and validity of the outcome measure before setting the sample size. Another example that also takes account of sampling costs appears in Chapter 7.

Difference in Two Means: Case 2

After substituting for the three other terms, solve the following equation for n:

$$\frac{Z_{1-a} + Z_{1-b}}{d} = \frac{(n-1)\sqrt{2n}}{2(n-1) + 1.21(Z_{1-a} - 1.06)}. \tag{6.8}$$

In this expression, the two Z scores have the same meanings previously assigned. The term "d" is the equivalent for means of the expression "h" used earlier. To calculate d requires a preliminary estimate of the variances of the populations from which the two samples were drawn. As a rule, this will be available from prior research; if not, it is worth taking a small preliminary sample to obtain estimates of variances and means of the two populations. If the population variances are the same, d may be calculated by:

$$d = \frac{\text{predicted difference in means by the threshold hypothesis}}{\text{common population standard deviation}}.$$

Otherwise, the denominator may be calculated by summing the two estimated population variances, dividing by 2, and taking the square root of the sum.

Illustrative Problem

A survey of male and female graduates of social work programs compared starting salaries of men and women graduates with the same degrees and prior experience (Crane, 1974). The procedures described in Chapters 4 and 5 were used to test whether the average difference in salary favoring men is at least $20 per month. This is the "threshold hypothesis value" — the minimum difference in means to be regarded as indicative of more than random fluctuations in the data. The protection against type 1 and type 2 errors was set at .75. These translate into Z_{1-a} and Z_{1-b} values of .77 (see Case 1). Here is the problem: How large a sample size will be needed if reliability of the measured difference is .90 and validity .88? The two population standard deviations are estimated to be $67 per month.

We first calculate $d = (20/67)(.88/\sqrt{.90}) = .28$, using equation (6.5).

Then the left-hand side of equation 6.8 becomes $(.77 + .77)/.28 = 5.5$. Solving the right-hand side for this value, we find that the required sample size is approximately 61. To obtain verification, substitute this value into the right-hand side.

RECAPITULATION

In summary, the outcome probability is a direct result of the falsity of the null hypothesis, the sample size, and the sample variances. Sample size is dictated by our decisions on type 1 and type 2 errors; sample variances are a function of the unreliability and invalidity of measures and the inconsistency of intervention effects.

Although our primary interest is in the effects of a social intervention, as measured by the falsity of the null hypothesis, we cannot afford to ignore the other determinants of our test result. We have now identified these and have seen how to take account of their effects. Putting this information to use in designing the evaluation will be the focus of Chapter 7. In Chapter 8 we extend our inferences to other parts of the value scale.

7 SQUARING RESEARCH DESIGN WITH POLICY REQUIREMENTS

The goal of this chapter is to demonstrate, with an example selected from the evaluation literature, the usefulness of the relationships set forth in Chapters 5 and 6 in designing an evaluation. Steps in the process are specification of values, development of outcome measures in terms of these values, value scaling of outcome scores, and use of the value scaling to arrive at a threshold hypothesis pivotal to subsequent design planning. The chapter will then show how to use this hypothesis and standards of protection against type 1 and type 2 error to specify sample sizes.

SPECIFICATION OF VALUES: AN EXAMPLE

An evaluation problem in the field of child welfare in Canada and the United States has been that of assessing the effectiveness of preventive services to families in which the children are deemed to be at substantial risk of physical neglect and abuse. The importance of this problem has been underlined by the growing body of research pointing to hazards to children associated with removal from their homes into foster care and by the recognition that the prevalence of neglect and abuse of children is much greater than had previously been recognized.

Interventions into family life, however benignly intended, illustrate the problem of value collisions characteristic of many social interventions. On the one hand they involve a possible threat to the privacy and autonomy of the families involved; but on the other hand not to intervene involves serious risks to the children.

97

The series of social work experiments begun in the 1950s by L. Geismar and B. Ayres (see Overton, Tinker, and Associates, 1957; Geismar and Ayres, 1960; ADP, 1969; Geismar, 1969, 1971) illustrate one attempt to resolve this dilemma. In these projects the interventions were made, but they were monitored as comprehensively as possible (Geismar and Ayres, 1960). The general rationale for the projects was that justification for the intervention would be strengthened if the intervention could be shown to be effective in improving family functioning and conducted in such a way as to support rather than invade families' rights. Effectiveness of the interventions was to be assessed by a series of field experiments, and control of the modes of intervention was to be secured through a process of training the intervenors and monitoring their performance (Overton, Tinker, and Associates, 1957).

Given the initial description of the families as at risk of problems of child neglect and abuse resulting in a need for foster care, effectiveness of the family services was broadly defined, at the outset, as reduction of these risks in treated families compared to a randomly assigned control group. This definition was elaborated into a set of conditions in various aspects of family functioning that were believed to be associated with high risk (Geismar and Ayres, 1960, pp. 10–20) and a scheme of assessment of change in these conditions (pp. 53–74).

MEASUREMENT DESIGN

Twenty-three areas of family functioning were identified; each one represents a related set of family tasks, such as the tasks entailed in securing health care, socialization of individual family members, and monitoring group cohesiveness (Geismar and Ayres, 1960, pp. 91–100). The twenty-three areas were scaled on the dimension of adequacy of task performance. Data are in the form of ratings. To guide the raters, detailed anchoring descriptions of inadequate, marginal, and adequate task performance were prepared. Task performance was assumed to be associated with risks to the children. Collectively, the twenty-three areas of task performance were believed to represent all aspects of family functioning having a bearing on the risks.

OUTCOME MEASURE

The Geismar-Ayres scale of family functioning is a battery of ratings applied by trained independent raters to reports of semistructured research interviews or narrative records of social work treatment. The ratings range from -3, inadequate family performance, to $+3$, adequate performance.

Details of the process of instrument construction and of the methods of data collection and scaling applied to the data are available in Geismar and Ayres, 1958. Our main interest here is in the outcome measure. In the Geismar-Ayres field experiments the outcome measure took the form of a series of differences in two proportions — for example, the difference in the proportions of experimental and control groups receiving ratings of better than "marginal" in a category of family functioning such as care and training of children.

MAGNITUDE ESTIMATION OF EFFECTIVENESS

As illustrated in Chapter 5, the Geismar-Ayres outcome measures may be used as input data for magnitude estimates of the effectiveness of family services based on differences between families receiving special preventive services and families not receiving such services. The estimates obtained from the sample of eighteen graduate students in social work described in Chapter 5 will be employed here to develop an illustrative evaluation design. To avoid repetition, the discussion is limited to one value scale. For more than one value assessment, the required sample size would be the largest one obtained by repeated application of the steps outlined herein.

Using the procedures of Chapter 5, an excellent fit to a straight line was obtained when the data were plotted on logarithmic coordinates. The closeness of the fit is shown by the r^2 value of .913, indicating correlation of .95. Extrapolating this line to the horizontal axis led to a threshold estimate of 8 percent. We interpret this percentage as the minimum difference between experimental and control groups that the student judges considered essential for effectiveness of a preventive program with high-risk families.

The best fitting line is described by the function:

$$\log(\text{effectiveness}) = \log(24) + .51 \log(d - 8), \qquad (7.1)$$

where d is the difference in proportions between the two samples already defined, 24 is an arbitrary constant estimated from the data, and 8 is the threshold value. This equation was obtained by use of a standard computer statistical regression program.

Expressed in original outcome scores, the equation takes the form:

$$\text{effectiveness} = 24(d - 8)^{.51}.$$

Thus, effectiveness was judged to be a power function of the percentage difference between experimental and control groups.

PATTERNING OF OBSERVATIONS

For the problem of assessment of the effects of a social intervention, the optimum pattern of observations is the one employed in the Geismar-Ayres series of studies. This pattern involves the identification of a population of families at risk and the random assignment of samples of these families to the experimental service and the alternative service; the latter is most often regularly available community services obtained by the families during the life of the experiment. The Area Development Project of Vancouver (ADP, 1969) and the previously cited study of aid to prisoners by Mallar and Thornton (1978) are good illustrations of the experimental method.

Although ethical objections have sometimes been raised to research in which service is withheld or experimentally varied, such an objection hardly applies to cases in which there is an absence of evidence as to the relative effectiveness of the different treatments. In all such cases, random assignment appears to be fair.

FORMULATING THE THRESHOLD HYPOTHESIS

In light of the earlier definition of a threshold effect as an 8 percent difference between experimental and control groups, take as the threshold and alternative hypotheses the following:

> *Threshold hypothesis*: the true percentage of cases whose child care is better than marginal will be at least 8 percent greater for treated than for control families.
> *Null hypothesis*: a zero difference.

The immediate importance of the threshold hypothesis lies in its being *the smallest difference we shall need to test* to establish whether the effectiveness of the services program is greater than zero. The smaller this difference, the larger the experiment needed to test the hypotheses. The threshold hypothesis is, as previously observed, pivotal to the evaluation plan.

DETERMINING AN OPTIMUM LEVEL OF PROTECTION AGAINST TYPE 1 AND TYPE 2 ERRORS

At this point we make use of the relationships among type 1 errors, type 2 errors, sample sizes, and the falsity of the threshold hypothesis set forth in

Chapter 6. From the small size of the threshold effect to be tested, one can already guess that large samples may be needed, especially if a high degree of protection against type 1 and type 2 errors is demanded.

The establishment of a standard of protection against errors is a policy issue, not a technical problem. It should therefore be dealt with by a group of raters using the method outlined in Chapter 4. The raters should be requested to consider, individually and collectively, a set of issues surrounding the selection of a level of protection against error. To help guide their decisions, they should be provided with data.

Issues to Be Addressed by Raters

The following is a typical list of issues surrounding the choice of type 1 and type 2 errors that a group of policy makers might be asked to consider:

1. Suppose that a type 2 error is made — that is, a decision that the effectiveness of a program is zero when in reality the program is effective. What are possible consequences of such an error and how important would these be for persons served by the program and for others indirectly affected by the problem of child neglect and abuse?
2. What if we make a type 1 error (that is, we decide that the program is effective when in reality it is not)? What are the possible consequences, and how serious would these be?
3. In light of the data supplied on the costs of experiments of varying sizes (Tables 7.1 to 7.3) and your views of the consequences of type 1 and type 2 errors, what is their relative importance, expressed as a ratio?
4. What probability should be designed into the evaluation of preventive family services of (a) avoiding a type 1 error, (b) avoiding a type 2 error?

Information to Be Supplied to the Raters

Making a decision as to the needed protection against type 1 and type 2 errors may be aided by several different kinds of information. One kind would be a summary of research on the incidence, prevalence, and consequences of the problem with which the social evaluation is concerned — for example, the problem of child neglect and abuse or of exposure to an industrial hazard. Another kind would be a statement of the rationale for the intervention to be evaluated.

A third kind of information is the costs of varying degrees of protection against type 1 and type 2 errors — information on the upper limit, per case, of research costs in view of budget projections. Costs may be expressed as the monthly costs of carrying out experiments of different sizes; these costs include sampling and net extra costs of treatment over the established treatment, and for research staff, facilities, and equipment. For our example, the Area Development Project of Vancouver, costs of the experiment (in 1969 dollars) were estimated to be $80 per month per case (ADP, 1969). This figure should be reduced by roughly one-half to allow for the costs of services that the experimental families would otherwise have received. Therefore, in our illustrative analysis, we use the cost figure of $40 per month per case. This calculation, it should be pointed out, ignores possible savings resulting from the experimental service, such as a reduction in the total costs of foster care of children in the community that would be achieved if the experimental intervention were effective.

A fourth type of information is the technical consultation services as needed. Projected sample sizes and costs of the evaluation are shown in Tables 7.1 to 7.3 for varying degrees of protection against type 1 and type 2 errors (e.g., probabilities of not committing these errors). These samples and cost estimates were arrived at in the following way:

1. Fix values of type 1 and type 2 errors (e.g., let these be $a = .10$, and $B = .10$). Then the degree of protection against these errors is defined as $1 - a$, and $1 - B$, respectively, for each type of error.
2. Using a table of percentiles of the normal distribution find the Z scores corresponding to $1 - a$ and $1 - B$, as in Chapter 6.
3. Using these Z scores solve equation 6.7 for n, with h, the effect size function, determined by the threshold hypothesis. Since our illustrative threshold hypothesis is to the effect that the experimental and control samples differ by 8 percent, we use a value of h equal to .20, which corresponds reasonably well to differences in proportions of .08 between two samples (see Table 6.2.1 in Cohen, 1969, p. 176). The resulting value of n is the required sample size.
4. Adjust h for the combined effects of unreliability and invalidity using the procedures given in Chapter 6. Then repeat step 3 using the adjusted value of h. This gives the required sample size adjusted for measurement error. For our illustration we assume that reliability = .89 and validity = .81.
5. Multiply the adjusted sample size by the monthly evaluation cost per case; in our example, this is $40. This gives the monthly cost of the evaluation.

6.   Repeat steps 1 to 5 for whatever combinations of $1 - a$ and $1 - B$ seem important. We use for illustration the following combinations:
   a.   Provide equal protection against type 1 and type 2 errors; the degree of protection ranges from a high of .95 to a low of .60 (see Table 7.1).
   b.   Fix one of these protection probabilities — say type 2 — at .90, and calculate n for various degrees of protection against the other (see Table 7.2).
   c.   Same, but fix type 2 protection at .80 instead of .90, and calculate n for various degrees of protection against type 1 error (see Table 7.3).

Judgments

For our illustrative problem we shall assume that the raters arrived at the following judgments:

1.   A type 2 error is a decision that the program is not effective by the standard initially decided on when in reality the program is effective by this

Table 7.1.   Sample Sizes and Costs of Evaluation per Month Required for Various Degrees of Equal Protection against Type 1 and Type 2 Errors

Protection against type 1 and type 2 errors	.95	.90	.85	.80	.75	.70	.65	.60
Required sample size (n)	544	327	211	141	90	54	29	12
Sample size adjusted for reliability and validity	725	436	283	188	120	72	39	16
Per month cost of the evaluation at $40 per month per case	$29,000	17,440	11,320	7,520	4,800	2,880	1,560	640

standard. Possible consequences of this error include the lost benefits involved in unnecessary search for alternative interventions and the withholding of services. Because of the possibly long-lasting effects of neglect and abuse on the children, this error must be considered extremely important from the standpoint of the children, but equally so for the parents, some of whom will lose an opportunity to learn to control or avoid neglectful and abusive behavior.

2. The major risks of type 1 error will be the perpetuation of an ineffective program and lost opportunities either to modify the program so as to render it more effective or to discover more effective approaches to the problem of the neglect and abuse.

3. Type 1 and type 2 errors both have serious consequences. These are roughly equal in importance, but somewhat greater weight is given to type 2 errors in view of the urgency of the problem of child abuse and neglect, the scarcity of effective means of dealing with this problem, and the importance of identifying promising approaches to it. Expressed as a ratio, the mean of the judges' ratios of the importance of type 2 to type 1 is 1.15.

4. To arrive at probabilities of protection against type 1 and type 2 errors the raters first considered some possible combinations: if protection against type 2 error is set at .95, protection against type 1 error is .95/1.15 = .83. The monthly cost in this case must be worked out by an application of equation 6.7; after adjusting the sample size for measurement error, this cost is $18,445. A less stringent standard of protection is to set type 2 protection at .90, whereupon type 1 error protection becomes .78. From a linear extrapolation in Table 7.2, we find that the approximate monthly cost of the evaluation will be $11,300. If we are willing to settle for protection against type 2 error of .80, we find that the corresponding value of protection against type 1 error is .8/1.15 = .696. From Table 7.3, we find that the monthly estimate is then $4,920.

5. These calculations illustrate the dramatic impact of protection against random sampling errors, coupled with protection against random measurement errors, on the cost of social evaluations. The raters decided that the costs of protection levels of .95 and .83 and .90 and .78, respectively, are more than can be budgeted for. Moreover, to secure samples of 300 cases in each group would entail carrying out the project simultaneously in several offices, a plan that would make it more difficult to maintain treatment consistency; dealing with this might well add substantially to the cost of the evaluation. On the other hand, the use of .80 and .70 standards of protection preserves the desired ratio between the two types of errors. The

Table 7.2.   Sample Sizes and Costs of Evaluation per Month Required for Protection against Type 2 Errors of .90 and Various Degrees of Protection against Type 1 Errors

Type 1 error protection	.90	.85	.80	.75	.70	.65	.60
Required sample size (n)	333	267	225	190	162	138	117
Sample size adjusted for reliability and validity	437	356	300	253	216	184	156
Evaluation cost per month at $40 per month per case	$17,480	14,240	12,000	10,120	8,640	7,360	6,240

level of certainty can be raised by rerunning the experiment if the results are borderline between effective and ineffective. With further testing it may also be possible to increase the reliability and validity of the measures, reducing the required sample sizes and hence the evaluation costs.

VARIATIONS IN THE RESEARCH DESIGN BY TYPES OF EVALUATON QUESTIONS

The experimental design used for illustration in this chapter is ideal for comparing the outcomes of different treatments. As shown earlier, outcome questions are only one of fifteen classes of questions to be considered. Questions concerning policy formulation, in particular, require a different

Table 7.3.   Sample Sizes and Costs of Evaluation per Month Required for Protection against Type 2 Errors of .80 and Various Degrees of Protection against Type 1 Errors

Type 1 error protection	.80	.75	.70	.65	.60
Required sample size (n)	141	114	92	74	60
Sample size adjusted for reliability and validity	188	152	123	99	79
Evaluation cost per month at $40 per month per case	$7,520	6,080	4,920	693	3,160

research plan from the plan appropriate for questions concerning implementation and outcome.

Questions concerning Policy Formulation

For questions about sources and mechanisms of influence on policy formulation, the research problem is to reconstruct a series of unique events that may have been distorted or concealed in the available records. The data needed for the value scaling operations described in Chapter 5 are rarely available. The research problem is much more like that of the historian or the jurist than the problems to which an experimental psychologist, for example, is accustomed. This is true as well of questions concerning the accessibility of the formulation process to citizens, the adequacy of needs assessment and of the impact model, and the extent of enactment of the policy. The last three of these problems require the application of specialized knowledge, namely of (1) standards of survey and needs assessment research in a specialized field, (2) the adequacy of an impact model in this field, and (3) critical differences, if any, in the policy as proposed and as enacted. Performance of these tasks depends not only on specialized research techniques but also on expertise in the substance of the specialized field.

Much more suitable research designs than the social survey or experiment are the professional review and the quasi-judicial inquiry (House, 1980, pp. 34–39). These designs have been employed extensively in higher education, medicine, and by government commissions.

The professional review study, as employed in higher education, for example, is carried out by specialists in subject matter areas. Standards of excellence on which there is general consensus among specialists are used to develop checklists of requirements against which particular programs can be compared. Standards of this kind exist for social research and can be applied to appraise need studies and impact models (Tripodi, Fellin, and Meyer, 1969; Fischer, 1978).

The evaluator's task is to identify teams of persons with the necessary background for whom there is no problem of conflict of interest and whose judgments can be expected to be independent. The evidence on which the judgments are to be made is the research reports and planning papers developed in the course of policy formulation. The *absence* of such evidence is of itself indicative.

The quasi-judicial method of inquiry is ideally suited to determine the facts of some past series of events. Its structure may or may not be adversarial (House, 1980, p. 37). It is, however, a method of dealing with evaluation problems for which the recorded evidence may be distorted and fragmentary and where there are identifiable opposing interests and points of view. The National Education Association in the United States has sponsored inquiries of this type into controversies such as the one that developed around the Michigan educational accounting system (House, 1980, p. 37; Patton, 1980, chapter 1).

The review panel is usually composed of prominent citizens or leading members of the professions involved. Typically, the proceedings resemble a court hearing, with verbal testimony before the panel acting as a tribunal. Rules of evidence are formulated. Opposed partisans are invited to present their cases. The aims of the proceeding are to facilitate (1) identifying all relevant issues, (2) placing each in context, and (3) obtaining a full range of evidence and opinions on each issue.

The scale and formality of the inquiry vary depending on the scope of the problem. Clearly focused on the five major policy formulation areas, this kind of inquiry can be rich in relevant detail and provide an essential context for subsequent evaluation of policy implementation and outcomes.

Questions concerning Implementation and Outcomes

Implementation and outcome questions differ fundamentally from questions about the formulation of a given policy in that they refer to recurrent events in dynamic systems. These questions are amenable to quantification, value scaling, and hypothesis testing. But instead of the single-shot experiments and surveys of traditional social science, they require the use of monitoring systems capable of repeating the evaluations at regular intervals.

The most useful monitoring devices are agency information systems. These serve as vehicles by which the data can be stored, retrieved, and analyzed. Findings of one set of evaluations are stored to become input data for the next set. Methods of analysis and inference suitable for this purpose are taken up in Chapters 9 and 10. The design and administration of agency information systems, a large and complex topic in itself, is outside the scope of this study. It has been treated exhaustively in several recent works; for a readable introduction, see Miller and Willer (1977), and for a book-length treatment, see Attkisson and Others (1978).

RECAPITULATION

In this chapter we have been primarily concerned with applying the relationships set forth in Chapter 6 in the construction of the major features of the evaluation design. These include the threshold hypothesis, which we arrived at by making use of the relationship we established between the outcome measure and the value scale; the patterning of observations, which for the present we limited to that of a straightforward random assignment of two groups; the levels of protection against type 1 and type 2 errors, which we arrived at through a process of consultation with a group of raters; and adjustment of the sample size requirements to allow for random measurement errors.

The comparatively simple design we have outlined is optimum for most evaluation problems. One of its major features — random assignment to experimental and control groups — may in some circumstances be difficult to achieve. Nevertheless, the gains from using this device, particularly the ease of interpretation of the findings, make it worthwhile to go to some lengths to find ways of using it. A more complicated problem of comparison, and observational designs appropriate to it, is discussed in Chapter 12.

THE PROBLEM OF GENERALIZING FROM POLICY EVALUATION

If the evaluation is an attempt to reconstruct a singular event, no problem of generalizing the findings arises. Whenever the evaluation is concerned with ongoing dynamic systems, as in appraising policy implementation and outcomes, the problem of the scope of permissible generalizations comes up.

The observations that are made result not merely from the policy variables on which the evaluation is to be focused but also from many contingent factors. These arise from three sources: the particular units sampled, treatments applied, and measurements taken. If the evaluation were to be immediately repeated, the results would not be the same. Most often, however, the effects of the accidental factors would be small and about as likely to operate in one direction as in another. To test that this is the case, the adequacy of research controls and the fit of the data to the assumed probability models may be checked.

To take account of the particularity of any set of observations, statistical hypotheses are tested. These tests serve only to put reasonable bounds of plausibility on the findings. They prevent us from taking any one set of observations too seriously.

The generalizations that they permit are to a population of statistical "might-have-beens," created by the very act of taking the observations. Call such a population a *local probabilistic system*. This population is the only one to which generalizations may, with safety, be made. But surely this is the population that matters: evaluations are undertaken to appraise *some particular realizations* of a policy, not the policy in some vague, more general sense. It is true that as evaluations are repeated in the same settings, a substantial body of information may be built up; but it is only good history. The ability to generalize to other policies and settings need not be increased by repeated studies. A preoccupation with such generalization stems from a confusion of policy evaluation with social science.

III OBSERVATION AND INFERENCE

8 PLAUSIBLE AND IMPLAUSIBLE HYPOTHESES

SPECIFICATION OF HYPOTHESES

As a pivot for the research design, a threshold hypothesis was formulated in Chapter 5 as the point at which the value scale becomes positive or negative. Although this hypothesis is undoubtedly important, it is only one of an infinity of hypotheses that could be tested. The ultimate objective is to arrive at a small plausible subset, composed of hypotheses sufficiently similar to be considered equivalent, and to downgrade all others as implausible.

A first set of candidates must be arrived at by reducing the infinity of points on the value scale (provided that this is more than dichotomous) to a manageable set. An obviously useful way to proceed is to make use of the calibration of the value scale developed earlier in Chapter 5. This method divides the scale into as many intervals as there are multiples of threshold effects. A hypothesis may then be stated corresponding to each of these points, all others not considered worth distinguishing.

The number of hypotheses needed will depend on the form of the value scale and width of the threshold effect. Zero thresholds are a special case; they may be expected for variables such as exposure to radiation for which it may be felt that there is no tolerable level. Division of the value scale into equal units is a simple scaling method applicable in this case.

Once selected, the hypotheses may be formulated in one of two ways. The simpler of these refers to sizes of differences — for example, between experimental and control groups. A limitation of such hypotheses is that they provide no evidence of where on the value scale the differences occur. After testing the initial threshold hypotheses formulated as a difference score, it is usually desirable to proceed to testing hypotheses that take the location of differences into account. This may be done by comparing different groups with a common reference point. Label this point a "baseline." It may derive from the average score or proportion of successes achieved by all groups in the experiment (in the case of two groups this is the point of no difference between them) or from prior research.

One may then formulate hypotheses in terms of the number and direction of threshold units by which each group departs from the baseline. Thus two hypotheses might be stated: (1) the experimental group is one threshold unit above baseline, and the control group is at baseline; (2) both groups are one threshold unit above baseline. Relative likelihood analysis, the main topic of this chapter, is especially useful for comparing plausibilities of hypotheses stated in this way.

THE MEASUREMENT OF PLAUSIBILITY

Evaluation almost always involves comparison of different sets of measurements. The effects index employed in Chapters 5–7 measures the size of differences. The threshold hypothesis test worked out in Chapter 7 was concerned with the significance of these differences.

Built into this test is a standard of plausibility, which is made up of three components: (1) an effect size requirement — the threshold difference; (2) an acceptable degree of protection against false positives — type 1 errors; and (3) a similar protection against false negatives — type 2 errors.

The outcome of the test is a division of the range of possible differences into two classes: plausible and implausible. Rejection of the null hypothesis, for instance, is in effect a decision that only differences of at least one threshold unit are plausible. Acceptance of the null hypothesis reverses this outcome: it is a decision that only differences smaller than the threshold 1 are plausible. These include the cases in which the differences are "in the wrong direction": the controls exceed the experimentals. Thus the effect of the significance test is to limit the range of differences deemed to be worth further consideration. Once this limit has been established, the analysis should proceed to reducing further the number of plausible hypotheses.

Reducing plausible hypotheses entails measuring the *relative plausibilities* of a collection of hypotheses that remain after the initial test. These should be formulated with reference to a baseline, as discussed in the previous section. By using relative likelihood analysis (Crane, 1980), each of these hypotheses is assigned a plausibility value between 0 and 1. Close consideration of these values, in conjunction with the evaluation problem, will usually lead to a reduction of the set to from one to three "best-bet" hypotheses on which policy making and further evaluation can proceed.

The remainder of this chapter is devoted to the technique of relative likelihood analysis. For simplicity, the comparisons are limited to one proportion (e.g., of "successes") and two groups. Only one statistical distribution — the binomial — is employed. In the appendix the analysis is extended to several proportions, three or four groups, and the multinomial, normal, and Poisson distributions; calculation procedures and computer programs for relative likelihood analysis are also given. Computer programs to extend this analysis further to the multivariate normal distribution are available from the author.

LIKELIHOOD INFERENCE

Whereas classical inference emphasizes the twin goals of hypothesis testing and estimation and Bayesian inference is a process of revising opinions in the light of data (see Chapter 9), likelihood inference is a search for valid means of weighing the relative merits of different hypotheses (Edwards, 1972, p. 2). Proponents of likelihood inference reject the classical interpretation of the significance test as a decision-making procedure (Kalbfleisch, 1975, p. 157). Given a properly designed research project, the prime purpose of statistical inference is to measure the relative support provided by the data for various possible outcomes, looked on as drawn from a universe of possibilities. Loss functions, decision strategies, utilities, and the like are not the business of the statistician. Developing improved methods of quantifying uncertainty is *the* major long-run goal for statistics —a goal that may be pursued without reference to practical applications. If likelihood inference is to be applied to practical problems, a connection to these problems must be made by means of a well-thought-out selection of hypotheses to be tested and research designs.

MAXIMUM LIKELIHOOD

In Chapters 5 and 6 the familiar binomial and normal model frequency distributions were used. Mathematical formulas have now been developed to calculate probabilities for many other models. These deal not only with the problem of counting discrete outcomes of chance experiments but also with cases in which the outcome of the chance experiment is a score on a continuous variable. Examples are the proportion of cases showing improvement over time in repeated sampling from populations of persons served by a social agency, or mean scores on standardized scales such as the movement scale (Kogan and Hunt, 1950) designed to measure various aspects of the changes in clients' problems over time. For social evaluators the significance of model frequency distributions lies in their capacity to describe the distribution of outcomes. Provided that the evaluator can assume or has demonstrated that a known probabilistic model fits the data, the model may be employed as in Chapter 6 to test hypotheses or to estimate magnitude of effects.

Suppose, for example, that a random sample can be drawn of persons who have applied to a family counseling agency for assistance with a problem of marital dissatisfaction (see Hudson and Glisson, 1976). The experimenter wishes to estimate the proportion of couples in the population who achieve a "norm" score on the measure indicative of a high degree of dissatisfaction. The binomial model may be used to calculate the probabilities of various outcomes and to estimate p, the population proportion, from P, the sample proportion. The probabilities of a number of hypothesized values of p may also be calculated, using the binomial model and the observed proportion in a sample.

The binomial probability model is given by equation (8.1):

$$C(n,x)p^x (1 - p)^{n - x} = P(E;p), \tag{8.1}$$

where n = the number of cases sampled; x, in the terminology introduced earlier, is the number of "successes," for example, the number of cases achieving the "norm" score on the marital satisfaction measure; and $C(n,x)$ is the number of ways in which x successes out of n trials can occur. $n - x$ is then the number of cases not achieving the "norm" score on the measurement. $1 - p$ is the proportion of "nonsuccesses"; $P(E;p)$ is the probability of x successes in a sample of n cases, for a given value of p, the population parameter. E refers to the observed sample: an "event" in a binomial probability process.

To simplify calculations, set $n = 10$ and let three "successes" be observed. This is the event E, the occurence of three "successes." Assume that the ten cases have been drawn randomly and that the value of p, the population proportion, is unknown. We wish to use the sample data to estimate p. Using equation (8.1), we can hypothesize any number of values of p and use each one to calculate $P(E;p)$.

A reasonable estimate of p is, of course, .3, the observed sample proportion. What is the probability of our observed $P = .3$ if the population proportion, p, is also .3? We can readily calculate this probability by substitution into (8.1):

$$\binom{10}{3}(.3)^3(.7)^7 = \frac{10 \cdot 9 \cdot 8 \cdot 7!}{7! \ 3!} \cdot (.3)^3(.7)^7 = (120)(.3)^3(.7)^7 = .267.$$

Natural logarithms may be used to evaluate this expression using the identity $\ln [120(.3)^3(.7)^7] = \ln 120 + 3\ln(.3) + 7\ln(.7) = -1.3211$. We then find the inverse of this logarithm, which is .267, the same result as we obtained above. This is the required probability of the observed data should the value of p, the population proportion, be .3. We can similarly find the probability of the observed sample $p = .3$ (or equivalently the probability of $x =$ three successes out of ten) for any other hypothesized value of p. Table 8.1 shows the probabilities of the observed sample data for ten other hypotheses, as well as probabilities for a second sample in which P is found to be .50. A good deal of variation is evident in the probabilities shown in Table 8.1. In both cases it will be observed that the largest probability of the sample proportion is for a hypothesized value of $p =$ the sample proportion. We shall soon make further use of this fact.

Generalizing from the examples shown in Table 8.1, we can summarize the steps that we followed: (1) the model probability distribution for the "experiment" of determining the proportion of cases meeting the norm for dissatisfaction on the Hudson/Glisson scale was specified as the binomial; (2) the experiment was carried out, two sets of observations of ten cases

Table 8.1. Probabilities That P, the Sample Proportion, $= .30$ and $.50$ for Selected Values of p, the Population Proportion, with $n = 10$

p					
P	.01	.02	.03	.04	.05	.10
.30	.0001	.0008	.0026	.0058	.0104	.0574
.50	.0000	.0000	.0000	.0000	.0000	.0015

p					
.15	.20	.25	.30	.35	.40	.45
.1298	.2013	.2502	.2668	.2522	.2150	.1665
.0085	.0264	.0584	.1029	.1535	.2007	.2340

each being taken; (3) the probability of the observed sample number of successes was calculated for various hypothesized values of p. This was done for both sets of data. In making estimates of p, the population proportion, from a sample of observations, it appears reasonable to regard as more plausible those estimates that tend to make the observed sample more probable. In the notation we have employed above, this amounts to selecting as best estimate the value of the parameter for which $P(E;p)$ is a maximum. In both of our illustrations this value of p was the observed sample proportion, P. P, therefore, is a *maximum likelihood estimate* (*MLE*) of p.

It is not always the case that the *MLE* is the sample statistic. There need not even be a unique *MLE*. But for sample means and proportions, with known model frequency distributions, and other statistics with which we are concerned in this study, there is always a unique maximum value of $P(E;p)$ or $P(E;u)$.

LIKELIHOOD FUNCTIONS

The foregoing calculations of the probability of an observed set of sample data involved the following essential elements: (1) the *model frequency distribution* determined by a population parameter; (2) a set of *data*, based on a random sample, from which a *sample statistic* was calculated. Using these elements, the quantity $P(E;p)$ — or more generally, $P(E;u)$, where u stands for any parameter of interest — was calculated. $P(E;u)$, it is useful to note at this point, is a probability and therefore obeys the addition and multiplication rules for probabilities (Spiegel, 1961, chapter 6) for different values of E when u is held fixed. This expression is generally read as "the probability of observed sample statistic E for hypothesis u."

It is possible to think of this expression as the likelihood of u in view of the observed event E. In this meaning the sample data are treated as fixed and the parameter as a variable, whereas in the first reading the parameter u was treated as fixed and the sample data E as variable. The second way of reading the expression treats it as a "likelihood" or a "measure of plausibility," whereas the first reading of the expression treats it as a probability. A more formal definition of "likelihood" will be provided, but as a preliminary working definition, use the phrase "measure of plausibility" or "measure of support."

Before proceeding to the more formal definition, we note another pertinent fact: in determining the *MLE* by the methods illustrated above, one would arrive at the same *MLE* *whether or not* the constant $C(n, x)$ was included. To put it another way, if the function $C(n,x) p^x(1 - p)^{n-x}$ and also the function $p^x(1-p)^{n-x}$ for the same data were graphed, the two curves would be of the same shape and have maxima at the same point; the first is merely a constant times the second — that is, at any point on the x-axis the value of the first curve would be equal to $C(n,x)$ times the value of the second. This would hold *regardless of the value* of $C(n,x)$; any constant could be multiplied in, for example, $1/[C(n,x)]$, without changing the relative shapes of the curves.

This leads us to a formal definition of likelihood: likelihood is a measure of the plausibility of a hypothesis concerning a parameter value for some specified model frequency distribution. It is measured by $KP(E;u)$, where K is any positive constant, E is a statistic calculated on a random sample, and u is a hypothesized value of the parameter. (See also the definition given by Edwards, 1972, p. 9).

The measure of likelihood that has just been described is known as the *likelihood function*. Although it is clear that this function is always mathematically related to a probability function or distribution, the two are not identical. The former does not range between 0 and 1, nor does it obey the addition rule for probabilities. The reason for these differences is that in calculating likelihoods, we treat the population parameter as a variable; in calculating probabilities we treat it as a constant.

The *ln* Likelihood Function

In calculating binomial probabilities for Table 8.1, we made use of the identity $\ln(a^n) = n\ln a$, which may be useful in simplifying computations of binomial likelihoods when these must be performed on a small calculator. A measure of likelihood sometimes employed is the *log likelihood function*, which is simply the natural logarithm of the likelihood function. When this function, sometimes referred to as the support function (Edwards, 1972), is employed, the arbitrary multiplication constant k becomes an arbitrary added constant — in view of the identity $\ln(a \cdot b) = \ln a + \ln b$. It is customary to adjust the value of the constant in such a way as to set the maximum of the log likelihood function — which we shall refer to as $l(u)$, where u will indicate some parameter — equal to zero. The log likelihood function will occasionally be used in this study as a computational convenience.

RELATIVE LIKELIHOOD

Ratios of likelihoods are of major importance to what follows and will now be considered in somewhat greater detail. For social evaluations their im-

portance lies in their usefulness as a measure of *relative plausibility*. By way
of illustration, using the data on Table 8.1 and for convenience setting $k = C(n,x)$, the likelihood, for the sample with $P = .3$, that $p = .20$ is .2013,
whereas the likelihood that $p = .30$ on the same data is .2668. The ratio of
these two likelihoods is therefore $L(.20)/L(.30) = .2013/.2668 = .7545$.
The hypothesis that $p = .20$ is thus about .75 as "likely" as the hypothesis
that $p = .30$. Using the above notation, this is given by:

$$\frac{L(.20)}{L(.30)} = \frac{KP(E;.20)}{KP(E;.30)} = \frac{P(E;.20)}{P(E;.30)} = .7545.$$

It will be noted that the constant K cancels out of this ratio.

As a convenient way of comparing a set of likelihoods for a parameter
such as p, calculated from a particular sample, we could take the ratio of
each of the likelihoods to one of their number. This would reduce them to a
common base or standard and thus render them more comparable. An obviously useful choice for the denominator of each ratio would be the likelihood $L(P;p)$ where P, as before, stands for the sample proportion. To
generalize this, we again write $L(E;u)$, where "E" stands for a statistic such
as a mean or a proportion calculated on a sample, and u stands for a
parameter. If we use $L(P;p)$ in this way, the value of the ratio for $L(P;p)$
itself will obviously be:

$$L(P;p)/L(P;p) = 1. \tag{8.2}$$

All other ratios calculated on the same data lie in the interval $(0,1)$. This
provides a convenient metric ranging between 0 and 1 for values of the likelihood ratios or relative plausibilities of different hypotheses concerning u,
the parameter. Label these quantities *relative likelihoods*.

Using log likelihoods, there is an exact equivalent of the relative likelihood measure. This is given by:

$$rl(u) = l(u) - l_{max}(u), \tag{8.3}$$

where $rl(u)$ = the log relative likelihood of a hypothesized value u of the
parameter; $l(u)$ = the log likelihood of u; $l_{max}(u)$ = the maximum value of
the log likelihood function.

It should be recalled here that $l_{max}(u)$ is obtained by using the observed
sample statistic in calculating the log likelihood, and that if we substitute
this value into equation (8.3), using the symbol $\hat{u}$ to represent the sample
statistic or *MLE*, we obtain $r(\hat{u}) = l(\hat{u}) - l(\hat{u}) = 0$.

It is not difficult to show, using our measure of the probability of a
sample statistic given by $P(E;u)$, that likelihoods from independent samples
may be multiplied together to obtain a combined or joint likelihood of a

hypothesized value of a parameter based on two or more samples (see Crane, 1980, p. 835).

Joint relative likelihoods may refer to different hypotheses for two or more samples — that is, that sample 1 is from a population with parameter value u_1, while sample 2 is from a population with parameter value u_2. This may be employed to evaluate the relative likelihoods of patterns of differences between experimental and control groups.

JOINT RELATIVE LIKELIHOOD ANALYSIS: AN EXAMPLE

A researcher has data from an experimental group and a control group, the former having received planned brief social casework (Reid and Shyne, 1969) and the latter having been placed on a waiting list. Part of the data from the experiment are proportions of the experimental and control groups that achieved a "benchmark" or norm score on a test of marital satisfaction. In the control group of sixty persons this proportion was .38, whereas in the experimental group of sixty persons it was .54. The experimeter would like to evaluate (among others) the following joint relative likelihoods:

1. That the control group sample is drawn from a population where the proportion, p, of persons achieving the norm score is .46, and likewise the experimental group. It will be noted that .46 is the mean proportion in the two groups, and the hypothesis is to the effect that the two population proportions are the same.
2. That the control group is from a population in which $p = .41$ and the experimental group is from a population in which $p = .51$. This will mean that the experimental population p is 10 percent greater than that of the control group, measured on the scale: experimental group proportion minus the control group proportion.

Using p_E and p_C for the experimental and control group proportions, respectively, and JRL to mean joint relative likelihood, JRLs that $p_E = p_1$ while $p_C = P_2$ are then given by the ratio:

$$\frac{L(E_1,E_2; p_1,p_2)}{L(E_1,E_2; P_1,P_2)} = JRL(p_1, p_2). \qquad (8.4)$$

Further extension of this formula to the three or more samples is straightforward.

Substituting the likelihood function for the binomial into the denominator of equation 8.4, we obtain, as the joint likelihood equation for two binomial samples:

$$JL(p_1,p_2) = p_1^x(1-p_1)^{n-x}p_2^y(1-p_2)^{m-y}, \qquad (8.5)$$

where p_1 and p_2 are the two hypothesized proportions; x and y denote the number of successes in each sample; n is the number of cases in the experimental group; and m the number in the control group.

To convert this to a joint relative likelihood function, we must take its ratio to its maximum, which occurs when $p_1 = P_1$ and $p_2 = P_2$:

$$JRL(p_1,p_2) = \frac{p_1^x(1-p_1)^{n-x}p_2^y(1-p_2)^{m-y}}{P_1^x(1-P_1)^{n-x}P_2^y(1-P_2)^{m-y}}, \qquad (8.6)$$

where $JRL(p_1,p_2)$ is the joint relative likelihood that one sample is from a population with parameter p_1 and that the other sample is from a population with parameter p_2.

To solve this example, we substitute the following values into equation (8.6): $p_1 = .46$; $x = 32$; $p_2 = .46$; $y = 23$; $m = n = 60$; $P_1 = .54$; $P_2 = .38$.

Conversion to the logarithms facilitates computation and gives us for the log of the denominator of (8.6):

$$32\log(.54) + 28\log(.46) + 23\log(.38) + 37\log(.62) = -81.40.$$

A similar calculation for the numerator yields -82.76, and to get the $jrl(p_1,p_2)$(using lowercase to indicate the log of the JRL), we subtract as follows:

$$-82.76 - (-)81.40 = -1.3587.$$

To obtain the JRL from the jrl, we look up the inverse of the jrl in a table of e, which gives us the value .26 for the JRL.

Maximum Relative Likelihoods for Departures from a "Baseline" Proportion

One form of analysis is to evaluate the joint relative likelihoods of each hypothesis for both the control group and the experimental group. With, for example, nine possible hypotheses for each group, this entails evaluating $9 \times 9 = 81$ pairs and may yield more information than is required concerning the control group. In such situations, it may be more useful to evaluate the joint relative likelihoods of a set of departures from baseline for the treatment group for the *most likely* departure of the control group from baseline. We simply evaluate the RL's or rl's of each departure of the control group from baseline and select the maximum from this set. We can then evaluate for each hypothesis concerning the effects of the treatment in which we are interested the quantity:

$$\frac{L(\text{max}) \text{ for the control group over the interval } [L,L]}{L(\text{max}) \text{ for the control group}} \cdot \frac{\text{likelihood of a hypothesis for the treatment group}}{L(\text{max}) \text{ for the treatment group}},$$

in which we have used $L(\text{max})$ as an abbreviation for maximum likelihood. This quantity is merely a particular form of joint relative likelihood, which may be designated as a *maximum relative likelihood* of *departure from a baseline proportion* or JRL_{max}.

To illustrate maximum relative likelihood, we use data from the Area Development Project of Vancouver (ADP, 1969, p. 66) on improvement in economic functioning of control and experimental group families. Improvement is measured by increased family earnings and by ratings of increased skill in money management. The data are as follows: of 92 families in the experimental group, 40 or 43 percent were rated as improved on overall economic functioning; of 121 control group families, 29 or 24 percent were rated as improved.

For these data a suitable baseline value, in terms of which the plausibility of hypotheses about control and experimental populations can be compared, is the proportion rated improved for the two samples combined. This is equal to $(69/213) \times 100$ or 32 percent (the sum of the number improved in each sample over the total of the two samples $\times$ 100).

Let the threshold value be 5 percent — the size of the experimental effect measured as a difference between the two populations, which will be taken to be significant. This difference represents about a 20 percent gain for the experimental population. Hypotheses to be tested are the points represented by four threshold units on each side of the baseline value of .32 — that is, .32 $\pm$ four threshold units = .32 $\pm$ .20. This is equivalent to the following list of percentage values: 12, 17, 22, 27, 32, 37, 42, 47, and 52 percent.

We decide to test each of these values for the experimental population *for the most likely one* for the control group population — that is, 22 percent (the one closest to the maximum likelihood estimate, i.e., 24 percent, of the control population percentage). Repeatedly applying equation (8.6) with the above hypothesized values substituted for the experimental group, and the value $p_1 = 22$ percent for the control group, yields the JRL's shown in Table 8.2.

Table 8.2.   Maximum Relative Likelihoods
of Nine Hypothesized Values of the Percent
Improved in the Experimental Population

Hypothesis	Maximum Relative Likelihood
12%	.00
17	.00
22	.00
27	.00
32	.05
37	.39
42	.84
47	.70
52	.23

On these data, any of the values 37, 42, and 47 percent improved seems plausible. These correspond to one, two, and three threshold units above the baseline of 32 percent. The evidence is that the treatment has made a significant difference from a policy perspective.

Further Examples

In Chapter 12 we apply joint relative likelihood analysis to data taken from reports on the Love Canal research. Additional social work examples are analyzed in Crane (1980). For practice in using the above methods, the reader may find it helpful to work through some of the numerical examples in the Appendix.

9 FLUCTUATING PARAMETERS

So far we have assumed that the underlying values of social policy variables are fixed; although sample values vary, the "true" values remain constant. This assumption has governed our selection of statistical inference methods. For many problems this assumption is unwarranted. Evaluation frequently involves monitoring the behaviors of large complex systems, such as workers compensation programs or nuclear power plants. The conditions of operation of these systems may alter in such a way as to change the outcomes with which evaluation is concerned. These changes may occur over time or place. In either case the "true effects," about which evaluative inferences are to be drawn, may be fluctuating. Under this condition the methods of statistical inference presented in Chapters 5–8 are inappropriate. Rephrased in statistical terms, population parameters for these problems are changing; like sample statistics, these parameters can be thought of as having frequency distributions — the form in which inferences must be expressed.

Monitoring activities are repeated at intervals. Each repetition is a form of analysis, the results of which are to be related in some way to the findings of previous analyses. We thus imagine a series of distributional expressions about outcomes, which are periodically consolidated and updated. The methods of inference we employ must not only cope with changing parameters but also take account of both the prior and the current information about the state of the system.

LOCAL PROBABILISTIC SYSTEMS

Evaluation often involves testing propositions about local probabilistic systems, the parameters of which may or may not be fixed, even over short intervals. Each evaluation is, therefore, a case study. But while replication in the traditional scientific sense is nearly impossible, repeated studies of a single system closely approach replication, especially if the system is in a relatively stable state. Although information about a program is never final, directions can be charted.

DIACHRONIC SAMPLING

Traditionally, social experiments and surveys create their probability systems through the devices of random sampling and random assignment — that is, instead of testing a probability model, the researchers collect data in such a way as to satisfy the postulates of probability theory. This procedure is so common that it may easily be mistaken as being the only one available. When working with data from an agency information system rather than traditional experimental or sample survey designs, simply taking cases as they come may be much better. It happens that episodes of service in agencies occur as random sequences over time. One may test the fit of a sequence of data to some known probability model. Once a model is identified, the test may be repeated at a later time to estimate changes in the parameters of the model. For example, after finding that the split-half exponential model fits case turnover data very well, one can employ it repeatedly to detect changes in case turnover. The only sample taken in this example is the collection of all cases closed, in the order in which they were closed, over a specified period. Holding the setting and data base constant, and studying changes over time in this way, has been labeled *diachronic sampling* (see Galtung, 1977, for a useful discussion of this and alternative ways of studying social systems).

The instability of effects and the availability of prior information considerably change our approach to threshold hypotheses (Chapter 5) and standards of plausibility (Chapter 8). Testing a threshold hypothesis makes good sense if the effect is stable; otherwise, it is more useful to formulate hypotheses in terms of probabilities that the effect lies within intervals of specified width. Call these credible intervals. Instead of setting sample sizes to guarantee some probability of rejection of a hypothesis that is sufficiently in error, we set them to guarantee that probability intervals for true effects are sufficiently small. In setting sample sizes we are able to consider not only the current samples but also the samples on which the prior distributions are based. This is an important gain in economy over the "single-shot" evaluation.

Finally, as with classical hypothesis testing programs, the required standards of sample size may not be achievable. This is usually the case during the initial exploratory stages of evaluation. The number of cases available is too small to enable us to identify a credible interval as defined earlier. A useful tactic to employ in this instance is to rule out as many hypotheses as the data allow. The stopping point in this process is looked on as only provisional since with more data, additional hypotheses could be ruled out. For clearly, if a small supply of data rules out an hypothesis, a large one will do so more decisively. As demonstrated below, a prior probability distribution of effects may be used to devise an optimum rule for ruling out hypotheses.

The key concepts of the Bayesian approach to statistical inference are introduced next and show how this system is especially well suited to diachronic studies. Then sources and forms of prior distributions are discussed, followed by a demonstration of how to combine information from the current sample with information about the prior distribution in order to update it. Later in the chapter Bayesian concepts are used to devise a decision rule for rejecting hypotheses that will minimize losses expressed in units of the value scale described in Chapter 5. This is especially useful with small samples.

BAYESIAN INFERENCE

This brief introduction to Bayesian concepts is indebted to Iverson (1970). For a readable, thorough, book-length introduction, see Phillips (1972). For more technical treatment, see Novick and Jackson (1974), and for examples similar to the ones introduced in this chapter, see Aigner (1968). Iverson suggests that the increasing popularity of Bayesian statistical inference reflects dissatisfaction with the classical inference procedures in which the rejection of the null hypothesis at best eliminates one possible value of the parameter, leaving an infinite number of other possible values. The power function could be employed to arrive at some idea of these, but more specific information is generally needed. Moreover, the power function is often difficult to obtain and is rarely reported in research. A case in which the null hypothesis is accepted is hardly more informative, again because the null value is only one of an infinity of acceptable values.

To cope with these difficulties, the Bayesian system of inference departs in a major way from the classical system in the definition given to a parameter. In the classical approach the parameter values are treated as fixed, and probability statements apply only to the sample. In Bayesian statistical inference the parameter is considered to be a variable and the sample fixed. Given this fixed sample, one makes probability statements about parameters, making use of Bayes' theorem about conditional probabilities.

Since the theorem is well known, its derivation will be omitted. Happily the derivation is quite easy and makes use of concepts encountered very early in the study of probability theory. Among schools of statistical inference, there is no dispute about the mathematical correctness of Bayes' theorem, only about the interpretation of some of its terms. To summarize the Bayesian interpretation of the theorem, begin with its equation:

$$P(H_k/D) = \frac{P(D/H_k)\,P(H_k)}{\sum_k P(D/H_k)\,P(H_k)}. \tag{9.1}$$

In this equation, as interpreted by Bayesian statisticians, H_k refers to a hypothesis concerning the parameter about which inferences are being made. The D in the equation stands for sample data. The right-hand side of the equation contains the term $P(H_k)$. This is the prior probability of hypothesis H_k. There is a prior distribution of all hypotheses representing the state of knowledge before the data for particular tests were collected. The summation in the denominator of the right-hand side of the equation may be stated in words as the sum of the probable sample values, each weighted by its prior probability. Again, this sum is a familiar quantity, but what distinguishes the Bayesian approach is the assignment of probabilities to hypotheses. This assumption is wholly foreign to the classical view in which there is no empirical counterpart, either subjective or objective, or a probability distribution of a set of hypotheses.

The left-hand side of the Bayesian equation is in the form of a conditional probability. In words this may be interpreted as the probability of hypothesis k given data D. Bayes' theorem is thus used as a means of merging data with prior information about a parameter. The outcome is a set of "posterior probabilities" expressed in symbolic form by the left-hand side of the equation. This may be described as the knowledge accumulated after the prior knowledge and current data are brought together. The data are used to "update" the prior probability distribution.

SOURCES OF THE PRIOR DISTRIBUTION

As noted above, the prior distribution must be provided by the evaluator before the data are collected. Use of the priors permits a cumulative approach to research; the posterior distribution from one study can be used as the prior in a subsequent study. The prior may reflect either data from previous investigations or merely the investigator's opinion concerning the distribution of the parameter. Bayesians differ in their views as to the grounds on which the parameter is considered to be a random variable. Thus, Iverson takes the view (1970, p. 90) that the parameter is fixed but is treated as a variable only because there is uncertainty about its true value. In this reconstruction the prior probability distribution represents merely the researcher's uncertainty. Aigner (1968), on the other hand, takes the view that the parameter is a true variable reflecting variations over a historical time. Either view, because the prior distribution is allowed to be subjective, may reflect only a particular investigator's opinions.

The implication is that the posterior distribution representing the outcome of some study might well be different for different investigators. One reconstruction of Bayesian statistics is to look on it as a system of personal inferences. This interpretation has been stressed in the most engaging book by Savage (1968).

In its mathematical aspects, the Bayesian system of inference is indifferent to the sources of the prior probabilities: they might, for example, be derived from previous research rather than from personal opinions. We limit ourselves to this case. In any event, Bayesians interpret the posterior probability as a measure of uncertainty in the researcher's mind concerning a set of hypotheses.

For the purposes of evaluation research, what is important about the Bayesian approach in addition to its emphasis on priors and cumulation of evidence is the form in which the results of an experiment are expressed. We now turn to a Bayesian treatment of the problems of evaluation of preventive child welfare services, which is treated in Chapters 7 and 12 from the point of view of classical inference.

Problem

A sample of twenty child welfare cases is drawn randomly, and five are found to show an increase in problems of caring for children after six months' service. The problem is to update and revise our past estimates of the proportion of cases showing "deterioration in care." Table 9.1 shows the data and calculations needed for a Bayesian analysis. The first column contains values of the parameter (in this case a proportion). These values have been selected by the researcher as of particular interest — a set of important hypotheses. The second column of the table gives the prior probabilities corresponding to each hypothesis. Note that these sum to one. Taken together, this set of values and probabilities constitutes the prior distribution. The third column gives the probability of observed sample values for each of the prior values of the parameter. Taking the first row as an example, the probability in the third column can be read as follows: if the prior probability is .03 (column 2), the probability of observing our five sample cases of "deterioration" is .032 (column 3). These "conditional" probabilities in column 3 have been obtained from a table of the binomial distribution, which is the model deemed to be appropriate to the data of the experiment. The reader may find it a useful exercise to look up in the binomial table the probability that $x = 5$ for various values of p, the parameter of the binomial distribution.

The fourth column of the table gives the joint probabilities of the sample data and particular values of the parameter. These joint probabilities are arrived at simply by multiplying column 2 by column 3. Note that this multiplication corresponds to the numerator on the right-hand side of equation (9.1). Column 5 completes the application of Bayes' theorem in that the joint probabilities of column 4 are expressed as a ratio of their sum, which is the denominator of Bayes' theorem. Note again equation (9.1). Column 5 is a set of posterior probabilities. This set may be interpreted as a revision in

Table 9.1. Bayesian Analysis of a Child Welfare Experiment

Prior Values of the Parameter	Prior Probabilities of Parameter Values	Conditional Probabilities of Sample Values	Joint Probabilities of Prior Values and Sample Values	Posterior Probabilities
(p^*)	Prob (p^*)	Prob (x/p^*)	Prob $(x \cap p^*)$	$Prob_1(p^*)$
(1)	(2)	(3)	(4)	(5)
.10	.03	.032	.001	.006
.15	.07	.103	.007	.039
.20	.20	.175	.035	.194
.25	.50	.202	.101	.562
.30	.20	.179	.036	.200
			.180	1.000

the corresponding prior probabilities given in column 1. The revisions are a result of the sample data. Thus we began with a prior distribution of parameter values and "updated" it by applying Bayes' theorem to a fresh batch of data. In this case the posterior distribution proved to be highly consistent with the prior distribution.

FORMS AND USES OF POSTERIOR DISTRIBUTION

To a Bayesian the posterior probabilities represent degrees of belief that have been changed as a result of an experiment. These could serve as a set of weights to be attached to each alternative in some proposed action scheme. For example, a policy maker might have to decide on a plan of allocation of funds among several alternative programs. Posterior probability for a threshold effect for a particular program might be an important factor in allocating funds to this program. One might express a set of preferences in quantitative form for the programs and then multiply these preferences by corresponding posterior probabilities of a threshold effect. The preferences could be based on cost. Multiplying by probabilities in this way might well change the preference ranking.

The form of the posterior distribution is of particular interest. Suppose, for example, that it is the normal distribution. This distribution is not only familiar but also has many convenient features: it depends on only two parameters, is symmetrical, and has been reduced to tables in many different ways. Consequently, a normal posterior distribution could readily be used to find the following:

1. Credible intervals for the parameter, corresponding to the confidence intervals of classical statistical inference; a 50 percent credibility interval is common in Bayesian analysis.
2. Variance: the variability of the posterior distribution, an important characteristic in deciding on the degree of "closure" attained by any particular study or series of studies.
3. As already noted, a set of priors for use in a subsequent study.
4. Probabilities to be used in some decision scheme involving an assessment of utilities and/or losses, as in the funding allocation problem.

BAYESIAN DECISION RULES

Although classical inference makes no attempt to formalize the decision process in mathematical terms, it is possible to reinterpret the significance test in terms of decision theory. Though this may be done in many different ways, a strong case can be made that the most useful of these is the one that is built on the Bayes' risk function as explained in this section (arguments to the effect that this is in a real sense the best approach are given by Barnett, (1973, pp. 224–26). Without giving a comprehensive treatment, we shall develop this idea with a simplified example.

As we have seen, a typical outcome of Bayesian inference is the posterior distribution on which credible intervals or other summary measures may be calculated. If we make use of a loss function as well as the Bayesian concept of a prior distribution of a parameter, we open a way to selecting a decision rule for statistical tests that seems superior to the rules available from classical statistical inference. At the same time we retain some essential features of the classical procedure, namely type 1 and type 2 errors of probabilities as basic considerations in selecting the test and determining sample size.

For illustration, return to the problem of deciding on the superiority of one treatment over another in reducing the risk of placement of children. Ordinarily an experiment of this kind calls for use of two groups, but we simplify the design by stating the problem in the following way: a well-established treatment in social work is known to produce satisfactory improvement (50 percent) of family service cases. A new treatment has been developed that is considered to be at least equal and very likely superior to the established one. To date this treatment has been applied in twenty cases chosen randomly. If there is satisfactory evidence from this sample of the superiority of this new treatment, a randomized field trial with larger samples, including one or two control groups, will be mounted. The problem on which this discussion will be concentrated is that of designing an optimum decision rule for choosing between two hypotheses expressed as follows: $H_0: p^* \leq .5$; $H_a: p^* > .5$, where p^* refers to the proportion of cases showing a satisfactory degree of improvement. The choice of .5 reflects the success rate of the established treatment. A "satisfactory degree of improvement" would be defined by use of the procedures set forth in Chapter 5. We also define the following terms:

Sample data: $n = 20$, the size of the sample; $x =$ the number of cases meeting the experimental criterion.
Decision rules: accept H_0 if $x <$ 9, 8, 7, 6, 5. These are a set of "critical values." Accept H_a if $x \geq$ the "critical value" in each case.

We thus have a total of five different decision rules for acceptance of H_0 and for its rejection (that is, the acceptance of H_a).

Value Score for Each Case

A simple value score for each case may be defined as follows: count cases that satisfy the value scale threshold as having a score of one and all others as zero. This procedure can be justified from past research in which it appears possible to measure change reliably (Kogan and Hunt, 1950; Geismar and Ayres, 1960) and also to arrive at reliable standards of change.

Finite Population

The finite population consists of families to whom the service might be applied, estimated to number 2,500. This estimate is derived from statistics concerning the number of "high-risk" families known to social welfare agencies over the course of five years in a particular community.

Prior Distribution of the Parameter

The prior distribution of the parameter refers to the proportion of families improving to the required degree. The following values, based on prior experience, are considered to be possible for this parameter: .20, .30, .40, .50, .60, .70, .80. In the Bayesian framework these values represent a set of prior states of nature to which a probability distribution corresponds.

Value Score for Each Service

The value score of a service is considered to be linearly related to value scores for cases. This is taken as only a working assumption since there has so far been little research in social work concerned with measurement of service values. The assumption of linear relationship is convenient but makes for a rather conservative measurement. Maximum value score for a service is equal to 2,500, the case in which all 2,500 cases in the population receiving the service achieve a case value score of 1.

Losses from Wrong Decisions

If p^* is greater than .50, and H_0 is accepted, loss in value scale units will be given by the formula $2,500p^* - 1,250$. This simply measures the difference between the value score of the new experimental service and that of the old service, which is known to have a 50 percent rate of achievement of the value scale threshold.

If p^* is less than or equal to .5, and H_a is accepted, the loss is given by $1{,}250 - 2{,}500p^*$. This is again the difference between the total value scores of the new and the old services. From these formulas, it is clear that the total value score depends on the value of p^*, the success parameter. Whether one gains or loses by adopting the new service depends on whether p^* exceeds the success rate of the old service — that is, whether p^* is greater than .5.

Loss Functions

Corresponding to each decision rule as just defined is a loss function defined as the amount of loss for each possible value of p^*. Since we have a prior containing seven values of p^*, the loss function will be a set of seven possible losses.

Expected Loss for a Decision Rule

Define p^* as a Bayesian parameter — that is, a random variable with a prior distribution. Then, in the usual way we may calculate its expected value by multiplying each possible value that it may take by the corresponding probability that it will take that value. The expected loss is then the sum of all these products. This is merely a weighted average, with the weighting factors being the probabilities.

An Illustration of a Calculation of Expected Loss

For illustrative purposes, use the decision rule $x \leq 8$, and the parameter values $p^* = .20$ and $p^* = .30$. This will give us two examples of losses. When $p^* = .20$, there can be no type 2 error, only a type 1 error since the hypothesis that $p^* < .50$ is true. Under these circumstances, the loss from a wrong decision is given by $1{,}250 - 2{,}500p^* = 1{,}250 - (2{,}500 \times .20) = 750$. From binomial tables we know that when $p^* = .20$, the probability that the observed number of successes will be equal to or greater than 8 out of 20 is equal to .01. The corresponding figure for the parameter value $p^* = .30$, arrived at in the same manner, is equal to .113. The total loss for a parameter value, $p^* = .20$, under this decision rule is equal to $1,250 - (2,500 \times .20) = 750$. The expected loss is $750 \times$ the probability that this loss will occur — that is, $750 \times .01 = 7.5$. By going through the same series of calculations for the parameter value $p^* = .30$, we find that the corresponding expected loss for that value of the parameter $= 56.5$. Then for any decision rule we can find as many expected loss figures as we have values of the parameter in the prior distribution.

Dominance

A dominant decision rule is one whose expected losses for each value of the parameter are least of a set of such decision rules in which we are interested. None of our rules is dominant, as calculating all expected losses would show. This creates a problem in selecting a best rule: since expected losses vary so widely with different values of the parameter, we have no grounds on which to pick any rule as superior to any other.

Use of prior distribution of the parameter and the Bayesian decision rule rescues us from this dilemma. The prior distribution is defined as in Bayesian inference: a probability function of p^*. We use the following prior distribution for our illustrative problem:

p^*	$Prob\,(p^*)$
.20	.05
.30	.10
.40	.10
.50	.30
.60	.35
.70	.06
.80	.04
	1.00

Bayesian Decision Rule

This is the rule having the smallest Bayes' expected loss — that is an expected loss over all values of p^*, when the total expected losses are weighted by the prior probability, $prob\,(p^*)$. Thus for the rule, accept H_0 if $x < 8$, the expected losses are 7.5, 56.5, 101, 0, 14, 2.5, .075.

Multiplying these by their respective probabilities and summing, to get the expected loss, we obtain:

$$(.05)(7.5) + (.10)(56.5) + (.10)(101) + (.30)(0) =$$
$$14(.35) + (.06)(2.5) + (.04)(.075) = 21.18.$$

By repeating this calculation for each decision rule we obtain the following complete set of Bayesian expected losses:

Critical Value	Bayes' Loss
5	58.58
6	48.87
7	29.07
8	21.18
9	20.35

The smallest loss is for the critical value (9). Therefore, we accept this as the optimum decision rule. We can then proceed to calculate the sample mean and apply this decision rule to test the hypothesis that the proportion that we are interested in is greater than .5 against the alternative that it is less than or equal to .5.

Some limitations of this example should be noted. First, the expected losses calculated for each value of the parameter are dependent on the sample size. This arises because we weighted them by the probability of a binomial sample of fixed size. Second, we have also ignored costs of sampling information and have assumed that the costs of the samples in the two programs were about equal. This seems reasonable since the samples present themselves for services and there is slight sampling cost attached to either program.

10 A CLASSIFICATION OF EVALUATIVE INFERENCE METHODS

This chapter outlines a classification of the inference methods dealt with in the last four chapters. The classification attempts to satisfy two principles: (1) subordination of techniques to value and policy requirements and (2) the assumption that there is no single method of inference applicable to all problems of evaluation. Keeping in mind the range of available options will enable evaluators to tailor their inference methods to the requirements of different problems.

OVERVIEW OF THE CLASSIFICATION

The primary dimensions around which the typology is constructed are the degree to which the evaluation variable (e.g., effectiveness, equity) has been scaled and the existence and nature of prior data.

Level of Value Scaling

The value scale is distinguished from the outcome measure employed, which is in most cases more specific and limited in scope. Nevertheless, the relationship between the two must be specified by a mapping process of some kind. In the simplest mapping scheme, two possible values of the value construct are provided for: either a minimally adequate effect has been achieved, or it has not. This can be applied separately to each case, as in the example given in the section on sources of prior distribution in Chapter 9. More often the minimally adequate effect refers to a threshold difference in proportions or means between the experimental and control groups. With such a simple two-point scale to work with, the evaluator makes use of a correspondingly simple set of inference procedures. We present several variations, which depend mainly on the way in which the hypotheses are formulated for a particular problem.

A second level of scaling of the value construct is that of a power function of the outcome measure being employed in the study. Essential features of this power function were presented in Chapter 5. The main advantage of using such a function of the outcome measure rather than the measure itself is that the value construct cannot as a rule be assumed to increase as a simple linear function of the outcome measure. Thus, in the child welfare projects discussed in Chapter 7, "effectiveness" is probably not related to "differences in percentage deterioration" in such simple fashion. The zero point on the two scales, for example, is unlikely to be the same: some prevention of deterioration must occur before "effectiveness" is rated to be more than zero. Moreover, a percentage decrease in the difference in percentage deterioration from 40 to 10 percent could lead to a disproportionate increase in "effectiveness."

It is useful to distinguish three types of mapping functions:

Equal: $x = y$.
Linear: $x = ay + b$.
Nonlinear: $x = ay^n$ where $n \neq 1$.

In a few instances, x, the values construct, can be scaled in monetary units, but this is rare in evaluating social services. Much more often it is necessary to use some method of scaling utilities or values, such as the method of magnitude estimation (Chapter 5). This method, which has been used extensively for judgment of such constructs as utility, poverty, seriousness of crimes, status, stress, and the importance of political office, offers one means of scaling values using as stimuli the scores on attitudinal and behavioral change measures. Here, the point is that the evaluator must be satisfied as to the level of scaling of the value construct that has been achieved before deciding on a method of inference.

Given a scale of any of the three varieties listed above rather than simply a threshold value, more detailed inferences become possible. These are of three main kinds: (1) plotting of outcome probabilities against the value scale; (2) point comparisons in the form of relative likelihoods that the parameter is in the close vicinity of selected points on the value scale (this could for example, be marked off in seven or nine equal intervals, the width of each corresponding to an "adequate" effect, as determined by evaluation standards and goals); and (3) in Bayesian analysis, comparing probabilities that a parameter is in different intervals.

Prior Information

The second main determinant of the choice of method of inference is the assumptions the evaluator is prepared to make concerning the prior data to be incorporated into the inference. There are two issues to be settled. The first issue is whether the parameter about which the inferences are to be made should be looked on as fixed or as a random variable with some calculable probability distribution. In most surveys and experiments taking place over a short period of time, parameters are considered to be fixed. In repeated studies on the same population (e.g., persons who receive social services of a particular kind) over extended periods of time, it may be more valid to regard the parameter as variable. This is analogous to inspection sampling in a factory, in which the conditions of manufacture may change in such a way as to change the proportions of defectives in a batch.

For rather different reasons, as we have seen, Bayesians interpret the parameter as a random variable. In their view, deciding whether the parameter is fixed or variable is not of any great interest since there is never any way of precisely knowing its value. Inference is a process of modifying opinions about plausible regions of the parameter. Almost by definition, these opinions vary. (The mathematics of inference are the same for those who take either view. This makes it possible to accommodate both views in the inference procedures presented in this chapter.)

The second issue on which the researcher must make a decision is that of the *existence* of prior information. Prior information may be available from previous evaluations, of which the present one is considered a replication. This view is characteristic of the classical and likelihood inference approaches. Using these approaches, one may begin data analysis by merging the present and previous samples (this must be preceded by some preliminary checking of the acceptability of the replication assumption). Then the analysis is conducted exactly as it was in the previous studies.

The Bayesian requires less prior information. Any source of information that enables one to construct a subjective prior distribution is acceptable — for example, medical records (Phillips, 1972, p. 72). Further examples are considered throughout the remainder of this chapter.

We now turn to a description of the typology of inference procedures based on joint consideration of prior information and measurement of value constructs.

NO PRIOR DATA; DICHOTOMOUS VALUE SCALE: CASE 1

In problems in this category no attempt is made to incorporate prior data into the inference. The outcome measure for the evaluation has been transformed into a simple two-point scale, indicating that a threshold has or has not been attained. Thus, in the child welfare example given in Chapter 9, each family case receiving service was classified as to whether a progress or change criterion had been met in the problems that were the focus of the services provided. Alternatively, the criterion can be formulated as a required difference between experimentals and controls in proportions or means.

Because of the simplicity of the evaluation criterion, problems in this classification lend themselves to inference procedures resembling those of the traditional significance test. Two variations of inferential procedure, which depend on the way in which the measures are applied and the hypothesis formulated, are presented.

Balancing Type 1 and Type 2 Errors: Example 1

The child welfare projects (Chapter 7) in which two samples were compared on proportions showing improvements, no change, and deterioration on the nine subscales of the Geismar-Ayres scale of family functioning may be used to illustrate this approach. We could replace the "measurable differences" and "greater change" yardsticks employed in these studies with a threshold or "minimally adequate" difference between experimentals and controls. This threshold may be arrived at by using a panel of raters, who would in an actual study apply their ratings to each of the nine subscales. Suppose, for illustration, the threshold turned out to be an improvement of 20 percent in the number of families showing "deterioration" in child care. This value can be used to establish an alternative hypothesis to be tested against a null hypothesis of no difference. Standards of precision and of certainty are established in the planning phase of the evaluation, as follows: if the true difference is at least 20 percent, the experiment must be sensitive enough to detect differences (that is, reject the null hypothesis in favor of the alternative hypothesis) with probability .90. Type 2 error is thus equal to $1 - .90 = .10$. Type 1 errors are considered to be about equal in importance to type 2 errors, and are therefore set at .10. Suppose further that a two-tailed test is decided on (Cohen, 1969, p. 3). Using Cohen's tables (pp. 191–92) with Cohen's effect size set at .40 translates into a sample size requirement of 120. Thus our sample sizes must be 120 in both experimental and control groups to satisfy the standard of precision and certainty previously established. Then the familiar test of a difference between two proportions could be applied to test the following hypothesis:

$$H_0: p_1 - p_2 < |.20|;$$
$$H_1: p_1 - p_2 \geq |.20|.$$

Assuming that the value scale is a simple dichotomy, no further testing would be required.

Relative Support for Pairs of Hypotheses: Example 2

In some cases interest may lie not so much in the differences between samples as in comparing the relative support for pairs of hypotheses as to the pattern of parameter values in experimental and control populations. Such an arrangement of hypotheses enables the evaluator to take account of the location as well as the existence of differences between experimentals and controls. With two samples and two hypotheses for each sample, four pairs can be arranged in the following matrix:

		Experimentals	
		Zero Effect	Threshold Effect
Controls	Zero Effect	JRL_1	JRL_2
	Threshold Effect	JRL_3	JRL_4

The *JRL* entries refer to joint relative likelihoods of the respective pairs of hypotheses. The simplest case is the one for two binomial samples. As in the first example for case 1, the *JRL*'s for each pair of hypotheses are calculated by use of the relationship:

$$JRL = \frac{\text{likelihood for experimentals} \times \text{likelihood for controls}}{\text{maximum likelihood for experimentals} \times \text{maximum likelihood for controls}}.$$

Each JRL has a value between 0 and 1 and may be interpreted as a measure of the relative plausibility, given the data, of a pair of parameter values in the control group and experimental group populations.

As in the previous example, the precision and certainty of the experiment should be determined at the planning stage, in accordance with the evaluation standards. If this has been done, the four JRL's can be treated, for policy-making purposes, as measures of the weight of evidence concerning outcomes of a social service. If cost data are available on the experimental and control services, the JRL's can be used to adjust the cost estimates for each service by the relative likelihood that a satisfactory outcome criterion will be satisfied.

PRIOR INFORMATION; DICHOTOMOUS VALUE SCALE: CASE 2

This case differs from Case 1 only in the availability of prior information. Several varieties of inference methods may be employed, depending on the form of the prior information. These are illustrated in the following example:

Balancing Type 1 and Type 2 Errors: Example 1

A simple case is the replication of a previous experiment in which type 1 and/or type 2 errors were set at a level too high to meet evaluation requirements. On the assumption that the parameter value remains fixed and that the second experiment truly replicates the first, the data from both may be pooled and the analysis conducted exactly as in the first example of Case 1. This procedure is analogous to sequential experimentation, with a stopping rule determined not by the level of significance achieved but by predetermined evaluation standards.

Prior Probability Distribution of the Parameter — Bayes' Loss Function: Example 2

Given a loss function (Chapter 9) and a sample size fixed, at least temporarily, by budgetary constraints, it is more useful to minimize type 1 and type 2 errors for the given evaluation resources rather than to fix them in advance. The simplest case is the one in which the loss is a linear function of the criterion measure. Then the analysis may be conducted exactly as in the child welfare example in Chapter 9.

Prior, But No Loss Function: Example 3

In the absence of a loss function but with a Bayesian prior showing the probability that the threshold will or will not be attained, the analysis may be conducted along straightforward Bayesian lines, leading to a two-point posterior distribution. This is illustrated by the child welfare example in Chapter 9. The posterior can be used to weight the cost per case of the two treatments.

One or More Replications; Parameter Assumed Fixed; Prior Experimental Data: Example 4

If the evaluator chooses to use a frequency definition of probability rather than the degree-of-belief definition embraced by the Bayesians, and also assumes that parameter(s) are fixed, relative likelihood analysis may be employed. The data of the original experiment and the replication are pooled, and a relative likelihood analysis is performed. Again, where two services are being compared, the *JRL*'s may be used to weight the cost data for each.

NO PRIOR DATA; RATIO VALUE SCALE: CASE 3

Case 3 is a direct extension of Case 1. A more complete scaling of the evaluation criterion has been achieved, expressed as a function of the particular outcome measure employed. For our purposes this function will be assumed to take one of the three forms given earlier. The transformed scale may be marked off in threshold score units and corresponding values of the outcome measure determined. If we suppose that this has been done to indicate three values of the evaluation criterion on either side of zero (for example, small, medium, and large), the scale will be reduced to seven intervals.

Relative Likelihood Analysis: Example 1

This example enables the evaluator to compare relative likelihoods of particular points on the evaluation criterion, such as no difference between samples or minimally adequate differences. This method is especially useful for comparing pairs of hypotheses as in Example 2 of Case 1. Instead of four comparisons, forty-nine may be made, consisting of all possible pairs of *JRL*'s over a seven-point scale for experimentals and controls. This provides a detailed map of relative support or plausibility over the region of experimental outcomes, which are important for evaluation. Not only differences between samples but also location of the differences along the continuum from "negative" to "positive" are preserved. With samples of adequate size adjusted for measurement error, the *JRL*'s will be sensitive to service effects, so that where these are present, there will be a clear elevation of *JRL* values in areas of the matrix closest to the "real" or "true" service effects. Where service costs per case are known, the JRL matrix may be converted to a matrix of costs weighted by relative likelihoods of various outcomes. Parameters are assumed to be fixed.

Significance Values for Differences: Example 2

Where the evaluation is focused on differences rather than on differences plus locations, it may be more useful to plot outcome probabilities against values of a difference parameter (e.g., between two proportions or means). Ordinary significance analysis may be employed for this purpose (an example is given in the next section; see also Figure 11.1).

PRIOR INFORMATION; RATIO VALUE SCALE: CASE 4

This case parallels Case 2, except for the more complete scaling of the evaluation criterion.

Parameter Assumed Variable — Bayesian Prior Available: Example 1

The most difficult condition to satisfy in this case is that of the Bayesian prior, which now must not be a simple two-valued set of probabilities but an entire probability distribution. Moreover, the application of Bayes' theorem must lead to a posterior distribution whose properties are familiar or calculable. This is a difficult technical problem, explored in detail by Phillips (1972). Once the prior and posterior distributions have been identified, a straightforward application of the method used in the child welfare example in Chapter 9 may be made. The posterior distribution can be marked off in a series of intervals corresponding to critical points in the value scale, and the relative probabilities that the difference parameter falls in each interval can be calculated.

Relative Likelihood Analysis: Example 2

This example is a direct extension of the example first considered to the case in which prior and present information is merged. In this case it is assumed that the current evaluation is a replication of one or more previous ones. Then the present and prior sample data can be combined.

IV TWO CASE STUDIES IN EVALUATION

11 TECHNICAL SKEW IN SOCIAL WORK EVALUATIONS

The need to bring together normative theory and empirical research can be placed in sharper relief by comparing it with evaluation as bare technology. In this latter form, abbreviated in this chapter as TECH, policy issues in evaluation design are reduced to problems of technique.

The thesis of this chapter is that this reduction to technique obscures implicit policy judgments; when made explicit, these seem to differ from what their authors intended. Therefore, the TECH form of evaluation has serious flaws. To explore its problems, two examples are analyzed in detail. These have not been singled out for their special weaknesses. Both were skillfully executed; they are good examples of an unsatisfactory form of evaluation.

ESSENTIALS OF TECH

Selection of Problem for Evaluation

Texts on evaluation in the TECH mode emphasize that evaluations serve a variety of purposes. These include, for example, management, policy making, and the testing of professional practice principles. No special priority is given to any of these purposes, nor to classes of special programs. Priorities are determined by what is known about a particular problem and especially by the availability of rigorous methodology. Whatever the goal, the key is a firm assessment (Rossi, Freeman, and Wright, 1979, p. 29). The specific goals are shaped mainly by the availability of rigorous technique; if technology permits, the goal is to assess impact; otherwise it is to monitor or describe.

Selection of Values by Which to Make an Assessment

Evaluators using the TECH mode make no attempt to construct a multidimensional scheme of values to guide planning. Instead, they negotiate a statement of program goals with policy makers and program managers. Their task is then to measure success in achieving these goals. This task is equivalent to routine selection of *effectiveness* as the guiding value.

Selection of Data Sources; Development of Measures

These are determined entirely by the policy makers' accounts of goals, subject to considerations of ethical and technical feasibility. Thus the Geismar-Ayres scale of family functioning (Chapter 7) evolved out of an outline for social workers' assessments of family problems (Geismar and Ayres, 1960). It is an operational specification of the social workers' goals.

Hypotheses

Hypotheses are unspecified; consequently, they are determined solely by the inner workings of the statistical inference black box induction machine.

Type 1 and Type 2 Errors

Type 2 errors are rarely estimated, never specified in advance. For type 1 errors, use is made of conventional magic numbers — the mysteriously potent .05 and .01. (The real mystery is the survival of belief in the magic numbers in the face of merciless exposures of their illogic, which began twenty years ago.)

THE PREVALENCE OF TECH

To obtain evidence of the prevalence of TECH, two collections of studies were examined. The first is a collection of all controlled field experiments in social work published between 1940 and 1970. The second is a set of seventeen field experiments published in the *Evaluation Quarterly* between January 1977 and January 1980. None of these was under social work auspices. They were carried out by social scientists from a variety of disciplines. In all, the two collections of projects published the results of 1,025 statistical tests.

All 1,025 findings were based on routine statistical inference embodying the essentials of TECH: use of null hypothesis of "no difference"; use of .05 or .01 levels of significance; omission of type 2 error specifications, selection and scaling of values, and explicit effect size (threshold effect) requirements. Although this survey is hardly exhaustive, it covers a period of forty years and includes studies from all of the social sciences. The complete uniformity of statistical method employed in these studies suggests that the use of TECH is predominant, if not universal, in evaluations that employ statistical tests.

TWO EXAMPLES OF TECH IN SOCIAL WORK RESEARCH

In Chapter 7 the main features of a design for the evaluation of preventive family counseling were developed. In this chapter two TECH-mode studies concerned with the same problem are explained.

The policy problem underlying these studies has been simply stated by Kadushin (1971): "What can be done to reduce the number of children coming into foster care?" (p. 34). In social work, a characteristic response to this problem is to provide case services to families in which there is deemed to be a substantial risk of neglect or abuse of the children. The services are designed to reduce the probability of deterioration of the caliber of the care of children to the point at which foster care becomes necessary. Two evaluations of these services are the Chemung County, New York, experiment (Brown, 1968; Wallace, 1967) and the Area Development Project of Vancouver, British Columbia (Area Development Project, 1969). Both studies employed randomized field trials, an advantage for this discussion in that use of this design tends to simplify the interpretation of findings. Though they were carried out on study populations with broadly similar characteristics, measured in the same way, and though the studies employed the same basic experimental treatment approach, their findings were inconsistent. This poses serious problems for the compilers of social work

Table 11.1. Improvement, No Change, and Deterioration in the Caliber of Child Care

Sample	Improvement		No Change		Deterioration		Total No.
	No.	%	No.	%	No.	%	
Vancouver treatment group	39	42.4	34	37.0	19	20.7	92
Vancouver controls	20	16.5	52	43.0	49	40.5	121
Chemung treatment group	13	27.6	24	51.1	10	21.3	47
Chemung controls	14	31.8	19	43.2	11	25.0	44

Sources: ADP, 1969, p. 66; Wallace, 1967, p. 385.

research findings (Maas, 1971). For our purposes the use of two sets of contrasting findings, however inconsistent, helps to bring out some often unrecognized determinants of the closure and statistical significance of research findings.

Table 11.1 displays for each of the two projects the data on the number of experimental and control group "high-risk" families rated as showing improvement, no change, and deterioration in child care during the period of treatment. The ratings were made independently by sets of raters applying the Geismar-Ayres measure of family functioning to narrative case material; this information was obtained from case records and by the use of research interviews.

PLANNED AND UNPLANNED FEATURES OF TECH-MODE DESIGNS

These examples of TECH serve to demonstrate that the consequence of leaving critical aspects of evaluation design unplanned is a reliance on standards of effectiveness and levels of type 2 error of which the evaluator may be unaware. To understand how this occurs, the planned and unplanned features of the design should first be distinguished.

Planned Features of the Research Design

In both projects objective definitions of the population to be studied using demographic characteristics readily identifiable from agency records were developed (Wallace, 1967, pp. 109–10; ADP, 1969, p. 64). Random sampling from these populations was carried out with great care. In the Chemung County study, after an inventory of families meeting criteria for inclusion in the project had been compiled, a table of random numbers was employed to assign cases to the demonstration group and the control group (Wallace, 1967, p. 110). Comparisons between the experimental and control groups were carried out to ensure that the randomization had not led to unexpected or unusual differences. Both projects made use of a second control group on which no initial measurement was taken; the effects of the measurement were shown to be insignificant.

Standardized scales were employed to measure outcome (though without norms). The Chemung County project made use of two independently administered standardized scales. These yielded similar results and provided evidence that the research findings might not be mainly the result of the measurement of procedures employed. To minimize systematic measurement error, independent, blind ratings of outcomes were obtained. Steps were taken to ensure that the research and treatment operations were independent.

An advantage of using measures tested in prior research was the availability of some data on their reliability and validity. The reliability (internal consistency) of the Geismar-Ayres scale ranged from .58 to .79 for different items on the test. Some data are provided on the concurrent validity of the Geismar-Ayres scale, from which it may reasonably be estimated to be between .5 and .6 (Geismar, 1971, pp. 15–28).

Unplanned Features of the Research Design

Effects of Sample Size.   In neither of the research reports is there evidence of calculation of the effects of sample size on the probability of statistical significance.

Random Measurement Error.   The term "measurement error" is used here to refer to both reliability and concurrent validity. The former will be used in its usual sense of consistency over items or persons or points in time, and the latter as correlations with a criterion measure. The effects of reliability and validity on the probability of statistical significance can be jointly or independently assessed. Joint assessment is more useful for our purposes; it is convenient to measure these joint effects by the extent to which observed differences between experimental and control groups are smaller than the true differences. This may be calculated as follows: true difference =

observed difference × square root of reliability/validity (Cleary, Linn, and Walster, 1970; for a fuller discussion, see also Chapter 6). Applying this adjustment to the Geismar-Ayres scale (estimating its reliability to be .78 and its validity .50), we obtain the following result:

$$\frac{\sqrt{.78}}{.50} = 1.76.$$

Thus, assuming that the estimates of reliability and validity are unbiased, an observed difference between experimentals and controls employing the Geismar-Ayres scale can be made more accurate by multiplying it by 1.76.

Inconsistency in Treatments. An important assumption of experimental design is that the treatments are fixed. This assumption is always violated to some degree in practice, but the importance of the violations depends on their degree. The effect is to increase the variation in outcomes within experimental and control groups. Consequently, standard errors of differences between the groups will be inflated, and the probability that any given true difference between experimentals and controls will lead to a rejection of the null hypothesis is reduced. There is, unfortunately, no simple method of adjusting the findings to allow for this problem. Boruch and Gomez (1979) proposed one such method, but its assumptions hardly seem realistic. (See Chapter 6 for a review of the method of adjustment employed in the ADP project.)

IMPLICIT THRESHOLD HYPOTHESES

After the threshold effect is specified, a standard of certainty may be defined for purposes of this study as a probability that, if the effect did in fact occur, the hypothesis of no effect will be rejected. This must be coupled with a specification of type 1 error probability. Then the standard is satisfied if both of these probabilities hold, and otherwise not; in this case, the advance specification of the two error probabilities amounts to a requirement of a minimum size of experiment. To meet the standard, we set the sample size in accordance with the procedures outlined in Chapter 7. These were not the procedures followed in the Chemung County and Vancouver projects. Instead, sample sizes and type 1 error were fixed, and threshold effects and type 2 errors (without regard to measurement error) were allowed to fall where they might. It can be argued that this amounts to using no threshold hypothesis as we have defined it. Nevertheless, if the threshold hypothesis is left unspecified, it becomes implicit as the minimum treatment effect needed for significance (examples of this quantity for proportion are given in Cohen, 1969, p. 183). By making a reasonable estimate of the level of type 2 error that would have been acceptable to these researchers, one can specify the implicit threshold hypothesis that they were using.

The policy requirement underlying the Chemung County and Vancouver studies was clearly that the services be effective in reducing the odds of admission of children to foster care. The research reports for these projects also make clear that the evaluators found it possible to articulate no statement in advance as to the size of the difference between experimental and control groups that should be required as evidence of effectiveness. The Chemung County researchers, for example, were able to come no closer to dealing with this issue than the following:

> But how effective can such a set-up be? We simply do not know, for similar programs have not been adequately researched. . . . The objective was not to place casework on trial (in the sense of asking whether it is desirable or necessary or in any or all cases effective), but rather to examine rigorously whether casework in a situation as described above would have measurable results in terms of the criteria employed. [Warren, 1968, p. 62]

This refers not to required effects but the effects to be predicted and reasonable aims for research. Given the lack of prior evidence, it is argued, research can aim only to detect "measurable results." "Measurable" in this formulation apparently meant to the researchers "large enough to be of practical importance."

The report of the Area Development Project employs similar language:

> Using the experimental model to assess the effect of the ADP treatment program we set up the hypothesis that integrated family services would be associated with greater improvement in family functioning in multi-problem families than in "usual agency services." [ADP, 1969, p. 65]

"Greater improvement" seems to be used here synonymously with "measurable results" to refer to any differences large enough to lead to a rejection of the null hypothesis.

It is not unusual for researchers to be reluctant to commit themselves in advance to standards of evidence. But TECH statistical inference procedures are definite and precise about these standards. A brief digression into the elements of TECH statistical inference is needed. Since these have been set forth in scores of introductory textbooks, no more than a brief outline of essential features is needed here. Use will be made of the brief formulation by Kalbfleisch (1975, p. 152).

A first essential feature of TECH statistical inference is an assumed probability distribution, such as the binomial or the normal. Also needed is a discrepancy measure (D) or test statistic, calculated on the sample data. An hypothesis is specified, and this, together with the discrepancy measure, is used to calculate a significance level (SL), defined as follows:

$$SL = \text{probability of a value of } D \text{ at least as large}$$
$$\text{as the one calculated from the sample.}$$

If the SL is "large," the data are taken to be consistent with hypothesis, and otherwise not. "Large" is conventionally defined to be greater than .05, or greater than .01. The hypothesis routinely tested for data of the kind shown in Table 11.1 is that the experimental and control group samples are from the same populations with respect to the quantity on which they are being compared. The alternative hypothesis is that the two populations are different. Literally interpreted, this alternative hypothesis implies that differences of any degree will lead to rejection of the null hypothesis. In reality, substantial differences need not entail rejection. If type 1 and type 2 probabilities are specified, the implicit threshold hypothesis is determined by factors described in Chapter 6 (sample size, the selected statistical test, unreliability and invalidity of measurement, variation in the dependent variable, and the consistency with which the treatment is applied). Data are available from our two exemplars on all but the last of these factors. We are therefore able to form upper-bound estimates of the probability of rejecting a hypothesis of no difference if it were false to varying degrees.

It is clear from the research reports that the Chemung County and Vancouver researchers were making a concerted effort to be definitive and rigorous — that is, to achieve a high degree of both precision and certainty. Not only the researchers but reviewers of the research were under the impression that the study had achieved a high degree of rigor (Zimbalist, 1977, p. 373).

Thus, one would expect that the researchers would have required, had they made it explicit, substantial certainty of detecting small effects. One could reasonably set this probability at .95, the same level they used for type 1 error. On this assumption the implicit threshold hypotheses that they employed may be expressed as follows:

Chemung County: to be considered effective, the treatment must produce true differences of 33 percent between experimental and control groups.

Vancouver Project: to be considered effective, the treatment must produce true differences of 23 percent between experimental and control groups. (These estimates were arrived at by determining the minimum difference necessary for significance, using equation (9.6.2) in Cohen, [1969, p. 403], multiplying by 1.76 to adjust for reliability/validity, and converting Cohen's h into percentage difference units.)

These are stringent requirements. Moreover, though the .05 level of significance employed in the reports of these projects leads one to think that they were employing the same standards of certainty of effectiveness, this was not quite the case.

TAKING ACCOUNT OF TYPE 1 AND TYPE 2 ERRORS

Even with error-free measurements and perfectly consistent treatments, inferences drawn from an evaluative study are uncertain. Uncertainty might be measured by the number and variety of relevant hypotheses that remain tenable at the conclusion of an experiment. For example, if there are three classes of hypotheses, corresponding to negative, null, and positive effects of an intervention, a study that has succeeded in ruling out any two of these would have made considerable progress in reducing uncertainty. But if all three categories of hypotheses remain tenable at the conclusion of the experiment, very little has been learned that is of use to an evaluator. Ruling in and ruling out of hypotheses is based, as we have seen, on some measure of the relative probabilities of the experimental results if the hypotheses were true.

The limitations of the TECH method of dealing with uncertainty can be made clearer by a detailed analysis of the stochastic uncertainty in the data of the Chemung County and Vancouver projects. Assume that we can fix in advance a series of intervals of effect sizes, bounded by hypotheses, H_0, H_1, H_2, and H_3, such that:

1. The *ES* (effect size: true effect of the treatment) specified by H_1 is minimally adequate from a policy point of view. Label *ES* values of size H_1 as "small."
2. H_0 represents an *ES* of 0, and all effects in the interval $[H_0, H_1]$ are regarded as too small to be of practical significance. A program that achieves effects less than those specified by H_1 is failing. (Note: read $[H_0, H_1]$ as "greater than H_0 and less than H_1.")
3. *ES* values in the interval $[H_1, H_2]$ are considered to be of small size.
4. *ES* values in the interval $[H_2, H_3]$ are considered to be medium; *ES* values equal to or greater than H_3 are considered to be large.

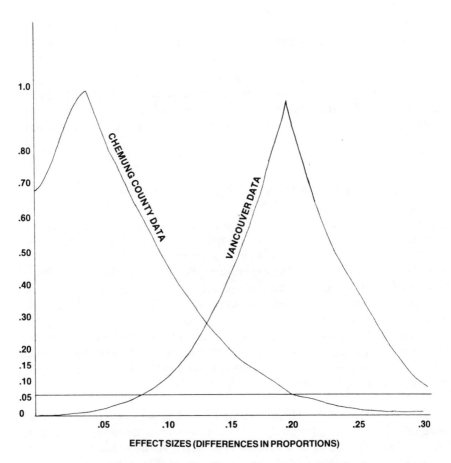

Figure 11.1. Significance Level as a Function of Hypotheses as to Effect Sizes. *Sources*: ADP, 1969, p. 66; Wallace, 1967, p. 380.

We could then compare *SL* values (as defined earlier) over each of these intervals. A simple method of doing this would be to plot the hypothesized *ES* values against corresponding *SL* values. For illustration, H_0, H_1, H_2, and H_3 might be interpreted as follows: H_0, no difference between experimental and control groups; H_1, an *ES* equal to one-third of the control group proportion; H_2, an *ES* equal to one-half of the control group proportion; H_3, an *ES* equal to two-thirds of the control group proportion.

Figure 11.1 depicts the relationship between *ES* values and the two-tailed *SL* (significance level), for the Chemung and Vancouver data. Though it is not precise enough to be used as a nomograph, it brings out some information that the TECH style of inference overlooks. For example, from the plot of the Chemung County findings, it can be seen that ignoring the possible effects of measurement error, an *ES* of zero and a "minimally adequate" *ES* have nearly the same *SL*, and are therefore about equally consistent with the data. In both cases the *SL* is large. If we accept as reasonable any value of the *ES* corresponding to an SL of .05 or greater, the Chemung County data are consistent with all *ES* values from zero into the "large" category.

From the plot of the Vancouver findings, it can be seen that while the largest *SL*s (say .40 or larger) are for *ES* values from "small" to "large," a range from "less than adequate" to "large" is consistent with data by the .05 critical value. Thus, the indeterminacy of the data is quite clear, and there should be much less risk of our overemphasizing any one hypothesis. Moreover, it is possible to use Figure 11.1 to compare the significance levels for any pair of hypotheses we happen to be interested in. Most important, the intervals of effect sizes should in an actual study be determined by policy considerations.

In TECH statistical inference, hypotheses are merely accepted or re-

Table 11.2. Ratio of Type 2 to Type 1 Error Probabilities in Eight Tests of Hypotheses concerning Family Functioning

Reference	Criterion Measure	Ratio of Type 2 to Type 1 Error Probabilities
ADP (1969, p. 66)	Percent of families showing no change or deterioration in family relationships	8.4
ADP (1969, p. 66)	Percent of families showing improved child care	8.8
McCabe (1967, p. 236)	Percent showing increase in rating of family functioning	12.6
Reid and Shyne (1969, p. 101)	Percent of families showing no change in or aggravation of problem	11.2
Reid and Shyne (1969, p. 139)	Percent showing overall improvement at six-month follow-up	8.7
Brown (1968, p. 124)	Percent of families showing no change or deterioration in family relationships	9.6
Brown (1968, p. 124)	Percent of families showing improved child care	12.2
Cohen and Krause (1971)	Percent of wives' reporting decrease in husband's drinking	9.2

jected. More information is obtained — that is, more efficient use is made of the data — when hypotheses are compared as to plausibility. Use of the .05 rule of decision making makes no distinction between a significance level of .06 and one of .94, as in the Chemung County data. This discards a good deal of information, which for an evaluator trying to make decisions about relative priority for different programs could be important.

Even if we are satisfied with the hypothesis of no difference between groups, TECH statistical inference ignores the problem of balancing type 1 and type 2 errors. As a result it is easy for us to become oblivious to the risks of type 2 errors, even for large experimental effects. Table 11.2 shows the ratios of type 1 and type 2 errors for eight representative findings from evaluation projects. The type 2 errors are calculated for true effects equal to one-third of the control group proportion. By almost anyone's definition, this difference should be taken as substantial.

The large imbalances of type 1 and type 2 errors seriously impair the usefulness of routine statistical inference for evaluation. This form of inference is like using a scale insensitive to differences of less than 100 pounds to weigh people.

12 A REANALYSIS OF LOVE CANAL DATA ON SPONTANEOUS ABORTIONS

THE SCIENTIFIC CONTROVERSIES

Love Canal is a 16-acre below-ground landfill located in the southeast corner of the city of Niagara Falls, about 1/4 mile from the Niagara River. Used for some thirty years as a disposal site for chemical wastes, it is now the site of a public elementary school and is bordered on two sides by single-family homes. In 1978, 95 families lived beside the canal; 410 students were enrolled in the school. The commissioner of health of New York State published in that year a report addressed to the governor entitled "Love Canal, Public Health Time Bomb" (Whalen et al., 1978). This report contained findings from a number of recent studies by the department of health, which had been undertaken as a result of residents' complaints of health problems from chemical fumes. The findings, in part, were as follows:

Eighty-two chemicals had been found in the landfill, including one known human carcinogen and eleven known or presumed animal carcinogens.

Unacceptable levels of toxic vapors were present in basements of homes bordering the canal.

Homes on the edge of the canal showed more evidence of contamination than homes across the street.

Observable surface contamination and signs of basement contamination were most pronounced in a number of homes bordering the landfill; air-quality data showed no such clear-cut differences.

It had been concluded that the landfill constituted a serious hazard to public health; plans had been developed to evacuate some 236 families from the area.

This initial series of investigations by the health department led to additional research on a number of problems, including reproductive abnormalities (Vianna, 1980), chromosome damage (Picciano, 1980), and nerve conduction (Barron, 1980, cited in Thomas and Associates, 1980). Research in these areas is still in progress. Associated with this research have been a series of scientific controversies. A brief review of the controversy over the data on birth abnormalities provides a backdrop for the work of this chapter.

Reproductive Abnormalities

The department of health studies dealt with miscarriages, birth defects, and low birth weights. The purpose of these studies was to compare the incidence of problems in areas of low and high levels of pollution near the canal and of Love Canal residents with population norms (Vianna, 1980). To measure variation in exposure, the residential area surrounding the canal was divided into five subareas on the basis of proximity to the canal and drainage. Two of the five areas were shown by this measure to have had the highest contamination. In these areas there were 158 pregnancies and 37 miscarriages; in the three areas of lower contamination there were 318 pregnancies and 35 miscarriages. These data show an excess in the miscarriage risk of about 113 percent in the higher-exposure areas; the rate in these areas was about 3.9 times population norms (Whalen et al., 1978, p. 15). The differences could not be accounted for by other factors known to be associated with miscarriages, such as age of the mother and pregnancy history.

Similar comparisons of rates of birth defects showed that in the higher-exposure areas there were 122 live births and 14 diagnosed birth defects; in the lower-exposure areas the corresponding figures were 280 and 15 (Bross, 1980, p. 728). The researchers concluded that these data were evidence of an increased hazard from exposure to toxic chemicals. Subsequently, the governor of New York appointed a scientific panel to review this study and others (Thomas et al., 1980). In its review the panel dismissed the above evidence as no more than suggestive, citing the smallness of the populations available for study and the lack of a matched population of controls (Thomas and Associates, 1980, pp. 21–22).

Commenting on the work of the scientific panel, a leading American bio-statistician attacked its procedures and conclusions.

His principal points were as follows:

1. The data base and controls were more than adequate; the latter exceeded the accepted standards for epidemiological field studies.
2. The group differences were large enough to indicate a very serious health hazard (e.g., a 113 percent increase in the risk of miscarriages and 114 percent increase in the risk of birth defects in the higher-exposure areas).
3. The panel had failed to make a rigorous assessment of the data; instead, it had relied on subjective opinions.

It was also pointed out that the panel was in a conflict-of-interest position, based on the following observations: the panel was reviewing the work of a department that was a principal source of funding for panel members' own research. The panel's report was shown to be critical of the previous commissioner of health but not of the present one. Criticism of current policies seemed warranted in that the department had spent $3.2 million for Love Canal studies and had produced only one article for publication, which had been rejected by the journal *Science* (Levine, 1980).

In spite of these latter controversies, the report of the scientific panel was widely heralded as having settled the question of health hazard at Love Canal. *Science*, it was generally believed, had shown that the worst hazard was the adverse psychological effects of premature release of inconclusive research findings and resulting government indecision (Holden, 1980; Smith, 1980).

THE QUESTION OF CONTROLS IN THE STUDIES OF BIRTH ABNORMALITIES

The brief comment on this problem made by the scientific panel (Thomas and Associates, 1980) referred to the need for comparability of control and risk populations. Bross's rejoinder was to the effect that this problem had been dealt with more than adequately. First, the populations studied were similar on socioeconomic characteristics, which might make for a difference in miscarriage rates. Specific factors known to be independently associated with birth abnormalities — age and previous pregnancy history — had been shown to be incapable of explaining the observed differences. Even more convincing was the fact that the rates of the higher-exposure group prior to moving to Love Canal had been low: out of fifty-seven live births there had been no miscarriages (Bross, 1980, p. 728).

Taking these points into account, Bross's argument that the controls were superior to current standards for epidemiological field studies seems persuasive. One aspect of this problem that needs further comment is the researcher's inability to control or measure precisely the degrees of exposure. Contamination is only an indirect indicator of this variable. Even accepting that it is adequate, a scientific study of the relationship of exposure to risk calls for data in the form of a continuous function extending beyond the range of its observable effects; the horizontal axis would be a measure of exposure and the vertical axis a measure of incidence. To use only two points on this horizontal axis, as the Love Canal researchers had to do, is to risk underestimating the strength of the effects. This is a consequence of the following principle: the smaller the interval employed, the less the explained variance. If the segment chosen happened to be equal to the variance in incidence attributable to measurement error, the explained variance and hence the observed relationship would be zero, regardless of its real strength (Hamblin, 1974, p. 88: Croxton and Cowden, 1939, p. 713).

If forced to compare only two points on the exposure axis, researchers would be less likely to underestimate the true relationship if they could compare a group with close to zero exposure with one in which exposure was substantial. How close they came to this cannot be conclusively judged. Fortunately, their data showing that the rates of abnormalities for their lower-exposure group were close to population norms (Whalen et al., 1980, p. 15) supports the assumption that they had captured a real difference between the groups. The most likely bias, if any, is in the direction of underestimation of difference in risks.

PLAN OF REANALYSIS OF THE DATA
ON MISCARRIAGES

An Index of Effects

As suggested, the scientific aspect of indexing effects is to model, as accurately as possible, the relationship between exposure and risk. Call the result the risk scale. This scale is then mapped onto a value scale of the seriousness of risk. Following the procedure proposed in Chapter 5, the mapping should be performed by a panel of citizen raters. Here an alternative procedure is used, based on Bross's suggestion that a 50 percent increase in risk constitutes a serious hazard. Bross points out that miscarriages are recognized as a sensitive early warning sign of genetic damage (Bross, 1980, p. 729). Extending his rating in both directions, we obtain the following scale:

From 0 to 24 percent — an insignificant risk.
From 25 to 49 percent — a significant risk.
From 50 to 74 percent — a serious risk.
From 75 to 99 percent — a very serious risk.
From 100 to 150 percent — an extremely serious risk.

A threshold value (see Chapter 5) is thus 25 percent of the lower exposure group percentage of 11 percent, or approximately 2.3 percent.

Type 1 and Type 2 Errors

There are reasonable arguments that both type 1 and type 2 errors should be set at a stringent level. The former is a finding of significant risk when the true risk is insignificant. The consequences of this error are likely to be that groups exposed to the hazard will experience increased stress (this process is examined in detail by Holden, 1980). Resources will be wasted in an effort to deal with a problem whose existence has been inadequately demonstrated. Therefore, a case can be made for a high degree of protection against this error.

The consequences of a type 2 error — failing to recognize a real hazard — appear to be even more serious. These include continued exposure of a large part of the population to unrecognized but serious risks. These risks seem especially serious if, as Bross suggests, reproductive abnormalities signal genetic damage. Therefore, although a stringent standard of protection against both types of error is required, tolerance for type 1 error can be somewhat greater. The following standards seem reasonable: tolerance for type 1 errors, 15 percent; for type 2 errors, 5 percent. Since the only difference that is of interest for policy making is $p_1 - p_2$, where p_1 refers to the more exposed population, a one-tailed significance test is called for (Spiegel, 1961, p. 169). The threshold value to be tested (.023 when expressed as a proportion) translates into a value of Cohen's h of .10 (Cohen,

1969, p. 176). Applying equation (6.7) with $Z_{1-\alpha} = 1.04$ and $Z_{1-\beta} = 1.29$ and solving for n, we find that sample sizes of 354 are required.

Are the available samples of 158 and 318 large enough for the proposed test? To determine this, we take their harmonic mean, given by:

$$n^1 = \frac{2n_1n_2}{n_1 + n_2} = \frac{2(158)(318)}{158 + 318} = 211.$$

This is well below the needed 354.

With the available samples we cannot test a null hypothesis that the proportions are equal at the desired level of type 1 and type 2 errors. Therefore, we are unable to use a satisfactory significance test to partition the hypothesized population differences into a plausible and an implausible set. An alternative procedure is to calculate a 95 percent confidence interval for the differences — that is, the interval within which we can assume with 95 percent confidence that the true difference lies. In tabular form, the data needed for this calculation are in Table 12.1.

The observed difference in percentages is $23.4 - 11.1 = 12.3$. The following expression may be used to find the 95 percent confidence interval:

$$P_1 - P_2 \pm 1.96\sqrt{\frac{(1-P_1)P_1}{N_1} + \frac{(1-P_2)P_2}{N_2}}. \qquad (12.1)$$

Substituting into this, with $N_1 = 158$, $N_2 = 318$, $P_1 = 23.4$, and $P_2 = 11.1$, we find that the lower limit is -4.7 and the upper limit 29.3 (see Spiegel, 1961, p. 159). This translates into percentage increases in the higher-exposure group over the lower of -38 and 238, respectively. To obtain more complete information on the plausible sizes of differences, relative likelihood analysis (Chapter 8) may be applied over the range of plausible differences.

Table 12.1. Miscarriage Rates by Residential Contamination Level at Love Canal

Births	Higher n	Higher %	Lower n	Lower %
	Contamination Levels			
	Higher		Lower	
Full term	121	76.6	283	88.9
Miscarried	37	23.4	35	11.1
Total	158	100	318	100

Source: Bross, 1980, p. 728.

RELATIVE LIKELIHOOD ANALYSIS

The method employed here is the one set forth in Chapter 8, in which the joint relative likelihoods of pairs of proportions in two groups were calculated. Each pair of values corresponds to a hypothesis; the relative likelihood (plausibility) of each hypothesis is to be evaluated.

The first step is to pick the pairs of values to be considered. As a first approach, take two threshold units on each side of P_2, the observed proportion in the lower-exposure group, and four on each side of P_1, the corresponding value for the comparison group. The narrower range selected for the first group is based on the fact that the sample is nearly twice as large as the other sample; therefore, it can be expected to provide more precise estimates of the population proportion. A more formal approach to this problem would be to employ a range equal to 1.96 standard error units on each side of both sample proportions. This would correspond to a 95 percent interval calculated for each sample.

Having selected the pairs of proportions to be included, use them to head the columns and rows of a two-way table, as shown in Table 12.2. Each square in the table corresponds to a pair of *JRL* values; the square is filled in by repeated applications of equation (8.6). A more detailed calculation procedure is given in the Appendix. Table 12.2 shows the results of this calculation. As to be expected, the *JRL* for $p_2 = .11$ and $p_1 = .23$, which are close to the sample proportions, is close to 1.0. This illustrates the principle of maximum likelihood that was discussed in Chapter 8. The table also shows that the largest *JRL*'s are concentrated within the ranges $p_2 = .09$ to $p_2 = .15$, and $p_1 = .19$ to $p_1 = .27$. Based on these data, it is useful to identify the most plausible miscarriage rates in each sample, rated on the scale

Table 12.2. Joint Relative Likelihoods of Selected Rates of Miscarriage in Two Groups of Love Canal Residents

Rates: Lower-Exposure Group	Rates: Higher-Exposure Group								
	.15	*.17*	*.19*	*.21*	*.23*	*.25*	*.27*	*.29*	*.31*
.07	.00	.00	.01	.03	.03	.03	.02	.01	.00
.09	.01	.06	.19	.37	.48	.43	.28	.14	.05
.11	.02	.12	.39	.76	.99	.90	.59	.29	.11
.13	.01	.07	.22	.42	.55	.50	.33	.16	.06
.15	.00	.01	.04	.09	.11	.10	.07	.03	.01

Table 12.3.   Most Plausible Miscarriage Rates, by Levels of Exposure
(Joint Relative Likelihoods Greater than .50)

Rates: Higher-Exposure Group (% Miscarriages)	Rates: Lower-Exposure Group (% Miscarriages)	Percentage Increase in High-Exposure Group	Rating of Hazard	Joint Relative Likelihood
23	11	109	Very serious	.99
25	11	127	Extremely serious	.90
27	11	145	Extremely serious	.59
23	13	91	Very serious	.55

of seriousness of hazard. Table 12.3 shows this rating for each *JRL* that is
at least half as great as the maximum one. Only four *JRL*'s are of this size,
and two correspond to a hazard rating of "very serious" and two to a rating
of "extremely serious." All represent increased percentages of risk in excess
of 90 percent. (It may also be noted that all four fall within the 95 percent
difference interval calculated previously.

To enable a comparison of the likelihood of these hazards with the
likelihood that the hazard is minimal or absent, Table 12.4 shows the *JRL*'s
for all pairs of proportions that differ by no more than the threshold value

Table 12.4.   Miscarriage Rates: Joint Relative Likelihoods of Increases of
Less than 50 Percent in the Higher-Exposure Group

Lower-Exposure Group %	Higher-Exposure Group							
	9	11	13	15	17	19	21	23
07	.00	.00	N.a.	N.a.	N.a.	N.a.	N.a.	N.a.
09	.00	.00	.00	N.a.	N.a.	N.a.	N.a.	N.a.
11	.00	.00	.00	.02	.12	N.a.	N.a.	N.a.
13	.00	.00	.00	.01	.07	.22	N.a.	N.a.
15	.00	.00	.00	.00	.01	.04	.09	.11

Note: N.a. = not applicable — increase is greater than 50 percent.

of .02; these are rated as "insignificant" on the hazard scale. It is clear from these findings that the *JRL*'s for these values are essentially zero.

IMPLICATIONS

Sample Sizes

Is the data base too small, as the scientific panel seems to have believed, to permit findings that are more than speculative? The effect of using larger samples would be to reduce the interval of plausible differences. This would leave the largest *JRL*'s where they are now — in the "very serious" to "extremely serious" range. It would not alter the above findings.

Seriousness of Hazards

The data strongly support Bross's contention that the hazard is serious. A more refined scale of hazard should be developed, but this seems hardly likely to reduce the above ratings. More likely, it would increase them.

Science and Social Policy

The Love Canal case illustrates the tension between scientific conservatism and the demands of social policy evaluation. To put this in another way, the scientific panel placed a very high premium on type 1 errors. The foregoing analysis suggests the need for a nonscientific (but not an antiscientific) balancing of these errors.

APPENDIX:
Evaluating Likelihoods Using an Electronic Calculator or the Computer

The researcher who periodically makes use of likelihood inference will find it advantageous to have calculation routines stored in a computer. Then data can be entered on cards or from a terminal, and RL's and JRL's can be calculated in a minute or two of total elapsed time. Data, as well as the program, may be kept in a file in the computer. New runs require only the replacement of the data in the file with a new batch. Because the amount of data needed is small, this part of the procedure is also very rapid.

If the researcher has no access to a computer, an excellent alternative is an electronic slide-rule-type calculator. This model of calculator has log, inverse and y^x functions, as well as a scientific notation capacity, which enables calculation with very small or very large numbers. With this equipment, RL's can be calculated rapidly, then multiplied together to form JRL's.

This appendix provides a set of routines for both calculator and computer for RL's or JRL's for the binomial, multinomial, normal, and Poisson model distribution — the models most frequently employed in practice. The routine may be stored in the computer and called up by a single command, such as $CONTINUE WITH (though this will vary from one installation to another). The advantage of the calculator is that it requires no knowledge of FORTRAN and takes very little time to learn.

For each of the model distributions, we first provide an example of a computation using a calculator and then display the corresponding computer program. The FORTRAN programs required are both elementary and short. The program for the binomial includes a plot of the JRL function. Sample runs are provided for the binomial and Poisson distributions.

CALCULATING JOINT RELATIVE LIKELIHOODS FOR BINOMIAL POPULATIONS USING AN ELECTRONIC CALCULATOR

Data

We shall illustrate the process by calculating two RL's and a JRL for a set of frequency data with corresponding proportions obtained from a hypothesized experiment involving a treatment group and a control group (see Table A.1).

Table A.1. A Binomial Example

	Treatment Group	Control Group	
Successes	10 (.45)	12 (.55)	22
Failures	12 (.55)	10 (.45)	22
Total	22 (1.0)	22 (1.0)	44

Baseline Proportion and Range of Hypothesized Differences between Groups

Assume that from prior research the baseline proportion is .50. Then set up an interval $[-L,L]$ over which to test hypotheses, in which $-L$ = (baseline $-$ .20) and L = (baseline $+$ .20). Thus $[-L,L]$ = [.30,.70] for our illustrative data. In an actual experiment we would, of course, have much larger samples and would test all of the hypothesized values in this interval. Here we shall test only two.

JRL

A joint relative maximum likelihood for the binomial model is the product of some hypothesized value of p for the treatment group and *the most likely departure of the control group proportion P_c from baseline*. For our data the corresponding value of the P_c is .50: this is the value in $[-L,L]$ for which the RL for the control group proves to be a maximum.

173

Calculation Equations

We may work in either likelihoods or log likelihoods. To begin with the former, the RL for the hypothesis that P_t, the treatment group proportion, is .30 is given by:

$$\frac{(.30)^{10}\,(.70)^{12}}{(.45)^{10}\,(.55)^{12}} = .31325$$

(see equation [8.2]) where we have used a calculator with a function y^x to calculate the four powers involved. The corresponding RL for the control group, for the value $P_c = .5$ given above is:

$$\frac{(.50)^{12}\,(.50)^{10}}{(.55)^{12}\,(.45)^{10}} = .91382,$$

where .5 is the maximum likelihood value for the control group over the interval [.30, .70]. The JRL is the product of these two values, or:

$$.31325 \times .91382 = .2862.$$

(See Equation [8.6].)

Log Likelihoods

If the samples are large and calculator has a log function but no scientific notation facility, it may be more feasible to employ the log likelihood function for the binomial:

$$l(p) = x\log(p) + (n - x)\log(1 - p).$$

For our data for the experimental group this becomes:

$$l(P_t) = 10 \log(.30) + 12 \log(.70) = -16.3198,$$

and

$$l(p) = 10 \log(.45) + 12 \log(.55) = -15.1591;$$

then

$$rl(.30) = -16.3198 + 15.1591 = -1.1607.$$

(See equation [8.3].) To get the rl, take $e^{-1.1607} = .3132$. This is identical to the value obtained by the method used above.

For the control group we have:

$l(pc)$ $= 10 \log(.50) + 12 \log(.50) = -15.2492,$
$l(\hat{p}c)$ $= 12 \log(.55) + 10 \log(.45) = -15.1591,$
$rl(pc)$ $= -15.2492 + 15.1591 = .0901,$
$RL(pc) = e^{-.0901} = .9138,$

which again is the same as was obtained by the method used above.

We now use a computer FORTRAN program to find a set of JRL's over $[-L, L]$ for these same data. As a first step we print out the FORTRAN program, which may, of course, use any corresponding set of binomial data.

PROGRAM: BINOMIAL LIKELIHOODS

This section presents a FORTRAN program to calculate and plot joint relative likelihoods of selected values of P_{11}, the proportion of successes in the experimental group for the most likely departure from baseline of P_{21}, and the corresponding proportion in the control group. The values of alpha, the log of the difference in odds of success in each group, are also calculated.

175

```
 1   C
 2   C      DIFFERENCES AMONG GROUPS : CALCULATE THE RELATIVE LIKELIHOOD
 3   C      FUNCTION FOR TWO SAMPLES USING THE FORMULAE GIVEN IN LINES 28,29
 4   C      AND PLOT THE GRAPH OF RB(P11,P21) : X-AXIS IS
 5   C      P11 VALUE FOR FIXED P21 VALUE AND Y-AXIS IS RB VALUES.
 6   C
 7          DIMENSION N(3,3),P(2,2),PHAT(2,2),AR(50),P11(50)
 8   C      WE PROVIDE STORAGE DURING THE RUN FOR THE NEEDED FREQUENCES
 9   C      AND PROPORTIONS AS WELL AS FOR MEASURES CALCULATED DURING
            THE RUN SUCH AS MLE'S.
10          LOGICAL*1 TITLE (80)
11          DATA N/9*0/,P/4*0.0/,PHAT/4*0.0/
12          READ (5,98) (TITLE(I),I=1,80)
13      98  FORMAT(80A1)
14          DO 2 I=1,2
15   C      WE READ IN THE FREQUENCIES IN THE 2 x 2 TABLE.
16          READ(5,1) (N(I,J),J=1,2)
17       1  FORMAT (2I5)
18       2  CONTINUE
19   C      NOW TO ADD UP THE TOTALS IN THE RIGHT HAND MARGIN OF THE TABLE.
20          N(1,3)=N(1,1)+N(1,2)
21          N(2,3)=N(2,1)+N(2,2)
22          N(3,1)=N(1,1)+N(2,1)
23          N(3,2)=N(1,2)+N(2,2)
24          N(3,3)=N(3,1)+N(3,2)
25   C
26   C      CALCULATE THE MLE'S FOR EACH GROUP.
```

```
27   C
28         PHAT(1,1)=FLOAT(N(1,1))/FLOAT(N(1,3))
29         PHAT(2,1)=FLOAT(N(2,1))/FLOAT(N(2,3))
30   C     READ IN THE PROPORTION P(2,1) WHICH IS THE BASELINE
     C     PROPORTION CALCULATED IN ADVANCE.
31   C
32   C
33         READ(5,3) P(2,1)
34   C     WRITE OUT THE TITLE OF THE JOB; THE TITLE WILL BE ENTERED,
     C     ACCORDING TO THE FORMAT GIVEN IN STATEMENT
     C     99,FROM A CARD THAT WILL BE INCLUDED AMONGST THE DATA CARDS.
35   C
36   C
37   C
38     3   FORMAT(F5.2)
39         WRITE(6,99) (TITLE(I),I=1,80)
40    99   FORMAT(1H1//1X,80A1//)
41         WRITE(6,7)
42     7   FORMAT(1X,' INPUT DATA FOR N(I,J)'//)
43         DO 6 I-1,3
44         WRITE(6,5)  (N(I,J),J=1,3)
45     5   FORMAT(1X,3I6/)
46     6   CONTINUE
47   C        WE NOW ARRANGE TO HAVE THE MLE VALUES WRITTEN OUT IN THE
     C         OUTPUT OF THIS JOB.
48         WRITE(6,4) P(2,1),PHAT(1,1),PHAT(2,1)
49     4   FORMAT(//1X,'P21 =',F5.2/1X,'PHAT11 =',F5.2,5X,'PHAT21 =',F5.2//)
50         I1=0
```

177

```
51   C
52   C
53   C        WE NOW READ IN A VALUE OF P11, FOR WHICH WE CALCULATE
              JRL'S FOR EACH OF THE 4 SUBGROUPS IN OUR EXPERIMENT.
54   C
55   10 READ(5,12,END=500) P(1,1)
56   12 FORMAT(F5.2)
57      I1=I1+1
58      RB1=0.0
59      RB1=(P(1,1)/PHAT(1,1))**N(1,1)
60      RB2=0.0
61      RB2=((1.-P(1,1))/(1.-PHAT(1,1)))**N(1,2)
62      RB3=0.0
63      RB3=(P(2,1)/PHAT(2,1))**N(2,1)
64      RB4=0.0
65      RB4=((1.-P(2,1))/(1.-PHAT(2,1)))**N(2,2)
66   C,C
67   C        TO GET THE JRL'S, WE MUST NOW MULTIPLY TOGETHER EACH OF
              OUR 4 RL'S.
68   C
69      RB=RB1*RB2
70      RB=RB*RB3
71      RB=RB*RB4
72      AR(I1)=RB
73   C        NOW TO GET VALUES FOR ALPHA, THE AVERAGE DIFFERENCE OF THE
              LOG OF THE ODDS.
74   C
```

```
75   C
76         P11(I1)=P(1,1)
77         ALP1=0.0
78         ALP1=P(1,1)/(1.-P(1,1))
79         ALP1=ALOG(ALP1)
80         ALP2=0.0
81         ALP2=P(2,1)/(1.-P(2,1))
82         ALP2=ALOG(ALP2)
83         ALPHA=0.0
84         ALPHA=ALP1-ALP2
85         ALH=0.0
86         ALH1=0.0
87         ALH2=0.0
88         ALH1=FLOAT(N(1,1))*FLOAT(N(2,2))
89         ALH2=FLOAT(N(2,1))*FLOAT(N(1,2))
90         ALH=ALH1/ALH2
91         ALH=ALOG(ALH)
92         ALH=ALH/2.0
93   C       OUR FIRST SET OF VALUES OF P11,RB,ALPHA AND ALPHAHAT (2)
             ARE NOW READY TO BE WRITTEN OUT.
94   C
95   C
96         WRITE(6,15)  I1,P(1,1),RB,ALPHA,ALH
97    15 FORMAT(1X,I3,3X,'P11 VALUE =',F5.2,3X,'RB(P11,P21) = ',F5.2,
98       *3X, 2(ALPHA1 =',F5.2,3X,' ALPHA HAT 1 =',F5.2/).
98.1 C       WE NOW REPEAT OUR CALCULATIONS FOR EACH OF OUR HYPOTHESIZED
             VALUES OF P11.
```

```
  99          GO TO 10.
 100  500     CONTINUE
100.1   C
100.2   C             CALCULATIONS ARE NOW FINISHED.
100.3   C
 101          CALL PPLOT(N,P11,ARI1)
 102          STOP
 103          END
 104    C
 105    C             THE LAST SECTION, WHICH IS OPTIONAL, IS A SUBROUTINE FOR
 106    C             GRAPHING THE JRL'S WE HAVE CALCULATED.  USE OF THIS OPTION
                      REQUIRES THAT THE COMPUTER INSTALLATION HAVE A COMPATIBLE
                      LIBRARY PROGRAM FOR PLOTTING, WHICH MUST BE CROSS REFERENCED
                      IN THE RUN CARD FOR THE JOB.

 107          SUBROUTINE PPLOT(N,P11,AR,I1)
 108          DIMENSION N(3,3),P11(50),AR(50)
 109          CALL SCALE(P11,I1,10.,XMIN,DX,1)
 110          CALL SCALE(AR,I1,10.,YMIN,DY,1)
 111          CALL AXIS(0.,0.,'P11',-5,10.,0.,XMIN,DX)
 112          CALL AXIS(0.,0.,'RB',3,10.,90.,YMIN,DY)
 113          CALL LINE(P11,AR,I1,1)
 114          CALL PLOT(12.,0.,-3)
 115          RETURN
 116          END
```

180

PROGRAM: "EXAMPLE RUN"

We now give an example of a run using our FORTRAN program binomial likelihoods and the data shown in Table 6.2. In this example the program is not printed out; only the results are shown. Superscripts in parentheses refer to additional explanatory notes at the end of the appendix. The data are in the computer disk file entitled "load." We list the data here to show their form and the fact that we have done certain minor computations beforehand. Observe that the arrangement of the data must correspond exactly with the format statements given earlier in the program.

```
#$LIST LOAD

      1        *******TITLE:EXAMPLE RUN****
      2(1)          10    12
      3              12    10
      4             .50
      5             .10
      6             .20
      7             .30
      8             .40
      9             .50
     10             .60
     11             .70
     12             .80
     13             .90

#END OF FILE
C    We are now ready to compile the FORTRAN program.
-$R *FTN SCARDS=S.PLOT2(2)
```

181

```
#EXECUTION BEGINS
 NO ERRORS IN MAIN
#EXECUTION TERMINATED
#$R -LOAD 5=LOAD
#EXECUTION BEGINS
```

```
*********TITLE:EXAMPLE RUN************

INPUT DATA FOR N(I.J)

     10     12     22
     12     10     22
     22     22     44

P21 = 0.50(3)
PHAT11 = 0.45        PHAT21 - 0.55
1   P11 VALUE = 0.10   RB(P11,P21)(4) = 0.00   2(ALPHA1) =-2.20   ALPHA HAT 1 = -0.18
2   P11 VALUE = 0.20   RB(P11,P21) = 0.02      2(ALPHA1) =-1.39   ALPHA HAT 1 = -0.18
3   P11 VALUE = 0.30   RB(P11,P21) = 0.29      2(ALPHA1) =-0.85   ALPHA HAT 1 = -0.18
4   P11 VALUE = 0.40   RB(P11,P21) = 0.80      2(ALPHA1) =-0.41   ALPHA HAT 1 = -0.18
5   P11 VALUE = 0.50   RB(P11,P21) = 0.83      2(ALPHA1) =0.0     ALPHA HAT 1 = -0.18
6   P11 VALUE = 0.60   RB(P11,P21) = 0.35      2(ALPHA1) =0.41    ALPHA HAT 1 = -0.18
7   P11 VALUE = 0.70   RB(P11,P21) = 0.05      2(ALPHA1) =0.85    ALPHA HAT 1 = -0.18
```

```
8     P11 VALUE = 0.80     RB(P11,P21) = 0.00     2(ALPHA1) =1.39     ALPHA HAT 1 = -0.18

9     P11 VALUE = 0.90     RB(P11,P21) = 0.00     2(ALPHA1) =2.20     ALPHA HAT 1 = -0.18

#EXECUTION TERMINATED(5)

#
```

EXTENSION TO THE MULTINOMIAL CASE: CALCULATION OF MULTINOMIAL LIKELIHOODS USING A DESK OR HAND CALCULATOR

The procedures we have employed to calculate binomial likelihoods using a calculator can be extended in a straightforward way to the calculation of multinomial likelihoods. The steps in calculation may be summarized as follows:

1. Given $m \times n$ table of frequencies, with one column for each group in the experiment, convert frequencies to proportions, using the column total as divisor in each case. The proportions and frequencies are shown in Table A.2.

Table A.2.   Findings of an Experiment Involving Three Multinomial Groups

	Treatment Group 1	Treatment Group 2	Treatment Group 3	Total
Problem worsened	20 (.13)	4 (.03)	2 (.01)	26
No change	72 (.48)	46 (.36)	31 (.23)	149
Problem alleviated	58 (.39)	78 (.61)	107 (.76)	243
Total	150 (1.0)	128 (1.0)	140 (1.0)	418

183

2. The proportions are the *MLE*'s for the population proportion in each cell.
3. From a statistical and mathematical point of view, the likelihood analysis for the binomial and the multinomial distributions are not essentially different: the *JRL*'s for each are obtained by use of the following equation:

$$JRL(p_{11}, p_{12}, \ldots, \text{all } p_{ij}) = \prod_{n=1}^{n} \prod_{j=1}^{c} \left(\frac{p_{ij}}{P_{ij}} \right)^{n_{ij}}. \qquad (A.1)$$

In words, this tells us merely to divide each hypothesized proportion by its *MLE*, raise the result to the n_{ij} power, (when n_{ij} is the corresponding cell frequency), and multiply together the results for all cells in the table. We perform this same calculation for both the binomial and the multinomial cases.

The binomial and multinomial cases do differ in the number of baseline proportions required: the binomial requires only a single baseline for each *JRL*, whereas the multinomial distribution requires $n - 1$ baseline proportions for each *JRL*, where n stands for the number possible outcomes of the experiment. The symbol "n" thus stands for the number of rows in a table. The reason for the requirement of $n - 1$ rather than n baselines is that once $n - 1$ proportions have been specified, the nth proportion is determined.

Example

These remarks can be illustrated by the data of Table A.2, where we use two baseline proportions, one for row 1 and the other for row 3. In each case the baseline is the mean proportion for the experiment as a whole — that is, for all three groups combined. The P_b for row 1 is .06, and for row 3, .59. Then we may hypothesize as follows: (1) Group T_1 will have 10 percent *more* "worsened" cases than baseline, (2) Group T_2 will have .05 of "worsened" cases, and (3) T_3 will have 0.01 of such cases. Similarly, (1) T_1 will have 20 percent fewer cases improved than baseline, (2) T_2 will have the same proportion as baseline (.59), and (3) T_3 will have 20 percent more cases than baseline (.79). The proportions for the middle category, "no change," are thus determined to be as follows: .46 for T_1, .36 for T_2, and .21 for T_3. This pattern of hypothesized results is shown in Table A.3.

Table A.3. A Set of Hypothesized Proportions for the Groups Shown in Table A.2

| | Treatment Group | | | |
Outcomes	T_1	T_2	T_3	Number of Cases
Problem worsened	.16	.05	.01	26
No change	.46	.36	.20	149
Problem alleviated	.38	.59	.79	243
Number of cases	1.00 (150)	1.00 (128)	1.0 (140)	418

We can calculate the RL of this by an application of equation (A.1). This yields the following quantities:

$$\left(\frac{.16}{.13}\right)^{20} \cdot \left(\frac{.05}{.03}\right)^{4} \cdot \left(\frac{.01}{.01}\right)^{2} \cdot \left(\frac{.46}{.48}\right)^{72} \cdot \left(\frac{.35}{.36}\right)^{46} \cdot \left(\frac{.20}{.23}\right)^{31} \cdot \left(\frac{.38}{.39}\right)^{58} \cdot \left(\frac{.59}{.61}\right)^{78} \cdot \left(\frac{.79}{.76}\right)^{107} = .312.$$

Note that with samples as large as those employed in this example, relatively small departures from the observed proportions result in *JRL*'s of less than .33.

For comparison, we calculate the *JRL* associated with a pattern of independence. The hypothesized proportion for each cell is then given by the expected frequency for the cell divided by the total number of cases in the corresponding group. This yields the set of proportions shown in Table A.4.

Table A.4. Proportions Corresponding to a Hypothesized Pattern of Independence of Groups for the Data of Table A.2

| | Treatment Group | | | |
Outcomes	T_1	T_2	T_3	Number of Cases
Problem worsened	.06	.06	.06	26
No change	.36	.36	.36	149
Problem alleviated	.58	.58	.58	243
Number of cases	150	128	140	418

We find that the *JRL* corresponding to this pattern of hypothetical proportions is less than 0.0000 after calculating

$$\left(\frac{.06}{.13}\right)^{20} \cdot \left(\frac{.06}{.03}\right)^{4} \cdot \left(\frac{.06}{.01}\right)^{2} \cdot \left(\frac{.36}{.48}\right)^{72} \cdot \left(\frac{.36}{.36}\right)^{46} \cdot \left(\frac{.36}{.23}\right)^{31} \cdot \left(\frac{.58}{.39}\right)^{58} \cdot \left(\frac{.58}{.61}\right)^{78} \cdot \left(\frac{.58}{.76}\right)^{107}.$$

The precise value of this expression is: 6.4458×10^{-12}. Thus the hypothesis of independence of the groups is highly implausible, compared to the pattern hypothesized in Table 6.4, the ratio of the *RL*'s being $.312/(6.448 \times 10^{-12}) = 4.84 \times 10^{10}$.

PROGRAM S.MULTI

This section presents FORTRAN joint relative likelihoods for two or three multinomial samples. It also includes the independence test as a special case.

```
C       WE RESERVE SPACE FOR A 3 X 3 TABLE OF FREQUENCIES, AND ALSO FOR
            CORRESPONDING TABLES OF PROPORTIONS AND VALUES.
C       WE ALSO ASSIGN VARIABLE NAMES AND TYPES INDICATE THE TYPE OF
            VARIABLE IN EACH CASE.  START EACH VARIABLE AT ZERO.

1       DIMENSION N(4,4),P(4,4),PHAT(4,4)
2       INTEGER RS(4),CS(4),GS
3       DATA RS,CS,GS/9*0/

C       Nr = NO OF ROWS (GROUPS)  VC = NO OF COLUMNS (RESPONSES)

C       WE MUST READ IN THE VALUES FOR NUMBER OF ROWS AND COLUMNS (3 IN THIS CASE)
            AND ALSO READ IN THE 3x3 TABLE OF DATA.
```

```
10   C
11         READ(5,100) NR,NC
12   100   FORMAT(212)
13         DO 11 I=I, NR
14         DO 10 J=I, NC
15         READ(5,101) N(I,J)
16   101   FORMAT(15)
17   10    CONTINUE
18   11    CONTINUE

     C     NOW TO READ IN A SET OF PROPORTIONS REPRESENTING THE PATTERN FOR WHICH
                 WE WISH TO OBTAIN A JRL.   AN EXAMPLE IS GIVEN BELOW UNDER "OUTPUT."

19         DO 13 I=1,NR
20         DO 13 J=1,NC
21         READ(5,102) P(I,J)
22   102   FORMAT(F5,2)
23   13    CONTINUE
24   C
25   C
26   C
27   C     TITLE:   PROGRAM TO GET JRLS FOR TWO OR THREE TRINOMIAL GROUPS.

     C     FIRST STEP:   ADD UP COL AND ROW TOTALS, AS WELL AS THE GRAND TOTAL.

28         DO 12 I=1,NR
29         DO 12 J=1,NC
```

187

```
30        RS(I)=RS(I)+N(I,J)
31  12    CONTINUE
32        DO 15 J=1,NC
33        DO 14 I=1,NR
34        CS(J)=CS(J)+N(I,J)
35  14    CONTINUE
36        GS=GS+CS(J)
37  15    CONTINUE

    C     NEXT, CALCULATE THE MLE'S FOR EACH PROPORTION:  THE

38        DO 16 I=1,NR
39        DO 16 J=1,NC
40        PHAT(I,J)=FLOAT(N(I,J))/FLOAT(RS(I))
41  16    CONTINUE

    C     NOW, THE RL'S AND THE JRLS

42        DO 18 I=1,NR
43        DO 18 J=1,NC
44        RM1=P(I,J)/PHAT(I,J)
45        RM1=RM1**N(I,J)
46        RM=RM*RM1
47  18    CONTINUE

    C     FIRST JRL CALCULATED, NOW DO THE JRL FOR THE HYPOTHESIS OF
          INDEPENDENCE OF GROUPS.
```

188

```
48    C

49    C      PROGRAM TO TEST FOR INDEPENDENCE OF TWO OR THREE MULTINOMIAL GROUPS.

50    C
51    C
52    C

53           DO 20 I=1,NR
54           DO 20 J=1,NC
55           RM2=FLOAT(CS(J)*RS(I))
56           RM3=FLOAT(GS*N(I,J))
57           RM4=RM2/RM3
58           RM4=RM4**N(I,J)
59           RMM=RMM*RM4
60    20     CONTINUE

      C      CALCULATIONS FINISHED, WRITE OUT FREQUENCY TABLE.

61           WRITE(6,499)
62    499    FORMAT(1H1/1X,'INPUT DATA TABLE'//)
63           DO 22 I=1,NR
64           WRITE (6,500)  (N(I,J),J=1,NC),RS(I)
65    500    FORMAT(/515)

      C      NEXT, WRITE OUT THE HYPOTHESIZED P's.

66    22     CONTINUE
```

189

```
67          WRITE(6,500) (CS(I),I=1,NC),GS
68          WRITE(6,501)
69    501   FORMAT(//1X,'PROBABILITY ASSIGNED PER CELL'//)

      C        FINALLY, THE TWO JRL'S, WITH LABELS.

70          DO 23 I=1,NR
71          WRITE(6,502) (P(I,J),J=1,NC)
72    502   FORMAT(/4F5.2)
73    23    CONTINUE
74          WRITE(6,504)
75    504   FORMAT(//1X,'ESTIMATED PROBABILITY PER CELL'//)
76          DO 24 I=1,NR
77          WRITE(6,505) (PHAT(I,J),J=1,NC)
78    505   FORMAT(1X,4F5.2)
79          CONTINUE
80          WRITE(6,506) RM,RMM
81    506   FORMAT(///1X,'RELATIVE LIKELIHOOD RM=',F10.6//
82         *1X,'RELATIVE LIKELIHOOD FOR INDEPENDENCE TEST =',F10.6////)
83          STOP
84          END
```

190

CALCULATING RELATIVE LIKELIHOODS FOR A POISSON MEAN USING AN ELECTRONIC CALCULATOR

The following calculations may easily be performed on any calculator having a natural logarithm function and its inverse. If these functions are not available, one can use the same sequence of calculations, looking up the values of these functions in tables of the natural logarithms and of e.

Problem

To calculate relative likelihood for the mean per sampling unit of a Poisson distribution. The sampling units could be towns or geographic areas of a given population. The mean could be the mean number of cases of leukemia or some other disease in the sampling units.

Relative Likelihood Equation

For convenience, we use the equation for the log relative likelihood of the Poisson:

$$rl(\text{Poisson}) = \sum_{i=1}^{n} xi \log u - nu = \sum_{i=1}^{n} \log \hat{u} + \Sigma xi, \qquad (A.2)$$

with n sampling units; the ith sample has x_i cases of leukemia; $\hat{u}$ is the MLE of the Poisson mean based on all samples combined; u is some hypothesized value of the population mean: we are interested in testing the relative likelihood of this value. The steps in calculation are as follows:

1. From the data, calculate $\sum_{i=1}^{n} xi$, the mean of the sampling means; $\hat{u}$, the mean of these means (or the grand mean); and nu, the number of samples times u.

2. Obtain the values of $\log u$ and $\log \hat{u}$.

191

3. Enter all values into equation (6.5) and solve for rl (Poisson).
4. To obtain its RLU, calculate or look up $e^{-rl(\text{Poisson})}$.

Example of a Relative Likelihood Calculation for a Poisson Mean

Data: Ten sample means are as follows: 1.0, 2.0, 3.0, 4.0, 5.0, 6,0, 7.0, 8.0, 9.0, 10.0.

Quantities Needed:

$$\sum_{i=1}^{n} xi = 55, \quad \overline{x} = 5.5 = \hat{u}.$$

Set u at 3.36.

Log Values:

$$\text{Log}(u) = \log(3.36) = 1.21194;$$
$$\text{Log}(\hat{u}) = \log(5.5) = 1.70475.$$

Log Likelihood: Substituting these values into equation (6.5) yields $rl(\text{Poisson}) = -5.70$.

Relative Likelihood: Take $e^{-(5.70)} = .003$. For comparison, we calculate the relative likelihood of $u = 5.49$, a value very close to the *MLE*. For this value, the *RL* is .999.

192

PROGRAM POISSON

This is a **FORTRAN** program to obtain relative likelihoods for a Poisson mean.

```
1    C
2         DIMENSION X(400
3         REAL*4 MU,LGRLU
4         DATA SUM,MU,XBAR,LGRLU,UBMAX,RLU/6*0.0/
5    C    XBAR=MEAN OF THE SAMPLE UB=THE BASELINE MEAN(RO BE READ IN)
6    C    UBMAX=MAX DEVIATION FROM BASELINE
6    C    MU=A HYPOTHESIZED VALUE OF THE POPULATION MEAN N=NUMBER OF CASES
7    C    LGRLU=LOG OF THE RELATIVE LIKELIHOOD
8    C
9    C    RIU=THE CORRESPONDING RELATIVE LIKELIHOOD FOR MU.
10   C
11   C              READ IN N AND BASELINE VALUE.
12   C
13   C
14        READ(5,100) N,UB
15   100  FORMAT(15,F6.2)
16   C    FIRST TO GET XBAR
17        DO 10 I=1,N
18   C
19   C
20   C              NOW READ IN THE DATA
20.5 C
```

193

```
21         READ(5,101) X(I)
22   101   FORMAT(F6.2)
23    10   CONTINUE
24         DO 15 I=1,N
25         SUM=SUM+X(I)
26    15   CONTINUE
27         UBMAX=UB+.20*UB
28         XBAR=SUM/FLOAT(N)
29         MU=UB=.20*UB
30   C          WE HAVE NOW SET MU AT THE FIRST VALUE IN  [-L,L]
31   C
32   C
33   C
34    20   LGRLU=FLOAT(N)*XBAR*(ALOG(MU)-ALOG(XBAR))
35         LGRLU=LGRLU-FLOAT(N)*MU+FLOAT(N)*XBAR
36   C
37   C
38   C              WE MUST NOW CONVERT LGRLU TO RLU
38.5 C
39         RLU=EXP(LGRLU)
40   C
41   C              WRITE OUT THE FIRST VALUE OF RLU
42   C
43   C
44         WRITE(6,500)N,MU
45   500   FORMAT(///1X,'NO IN THE SAMPLE=',15//1X, HYPOTHESIZED MU=',F10.3)
46         WRITE(6,501) XBAR,UB,RLU
```

194

```
47   501 FORMAT(//1X,'SAMPLE MEAN=',F10.3//
48      *1X,'BASELINE MEAN=',F10.3//
49      *1X,'RELATIVE LIKELIHOOD OF MU=',F10.3///)
50   C
51   C
52   C            NOW DO THE NEXT VALUE OF RLU
53   C
54   C
55       MU=MU+.05*UB
56       IF(MU.GE.UBMAX) GO TO 30
57       GO TO 20
58   C
59   C
60   C
61   C            WRITE OUT THE INPUT DATA
62   C
63   C
64   C
65   30  WRITE(6,510)(X(I),I=1,N)
65.1 510 FORMAT(1X,'INPUT DATA'//(1X,10F6.2))
66       STOP
67       END
```

195

PROGRAM POISSON: A SAMPLE RUN

This is a computer run from a terminal using FORTRAN program "Poisson."

```
        $R *FTN SCARDS=POISSON(6)

#EXECUTION BEGINS
 NO ERRORS IN MAIN
#EXECUTION TERMINATED
#
        $R -LOAD 5=DATA(7)

#EXECUTION BEGINS

 NO IN THE SAMPLE= 10
 HYPOTHESIZED MU= 4.000
 SAMPLE MEAN= 5.500
 BASELINE MEAN= 5.000
 RELATIVE LIKELIHOOD OF MU= 0.081

 NO IN THE SAMPLE= 10
 HYPOTHESIZED MU= 4.250
 SAMPLE MEAN= 5.500
 BASELINE MEAN= 5.000
 RELATIVE LIKELIHOOD OF MU= 0.186

 NO IN THE SAMPLE= 10
 HYPOTHESIZED MU= 4.500
 SAMPLE MEAN= 5.500
```

BASELINE MEAN= 5.000
RELATIVE LIKELIHOOD OF MU= 0.355

NO IN THE SAMPLE= 10
HYPOTHESIZED MU= 4.750
SAMPLE MEAN= 5.500
BASELINE MEAN= 5.000
RELATIVE LIKELIHOOD OF MU= 0.569

NO IN THE SAMPLE= 10
HYPOTHESIZED MU= 5.000
SAMPLE MEAN= 5.500
BASELINE MEAN= 5.000
RELATIVE LIKELIHOOD OF MU= 0.785

NO IN THE SAMPLE= 10
HYPOTHESIZED MU= 5.250
SAMPLE MEAN= 5.500
BASELINE MEAN= 5.000
RELATIVE LIKELIHOOD OF MU= 0.943

NO IN THE SAMPLE= 10
HYPOTHESIZED MU= 5.750
SAMPLE MEAN= 5.500
BASELINE MEAN= 5.000
RELATIVE LIKELIHOOD OF MU= 0.946

NO IN THE SAMPLE= 10
HYPOTHESIZED MU= 6.000

```
SAMPLE MEAN= 5.500
BASELINE MEAN= 5.000
RELATIVE LIKELIHOOD OF MU= 0.807
```

CALCULATION OF THE MAXIMUM RELATIVE LIKELIHOOD FOR THE MEAN OF A NORMAL SAMPLE USING AN ELECTRONIC CALCULATOR

Problem

We are given a sample of N observations known or assumed to be from a $N(u,\sigma)$ distribution, that is a normal distribution with a mean of u and standard deviation of σ. The problem is to find the maximum relative likelihood (MRL) of mu, a hypothesized value of u, for the *maximum likelihood estimate of σ*, the population standard deviation. Given n such samples, experimentally independent, we can calculate the JRL's of a set of n hypotheses concerning the population means by multiplying together the n MRL's. (We use the term MRL to indicate a two-parameter likelihood that has been maximized over one of the parameters.)

MRL Equation

We make use of equation:

$$MRL = \left[\, 1 + \frac{(\overline{x}-mu)^2}{(\hat\sigma)} \,\right]^{-\frac{n}{2}}, \tag{A.3}$$

in which the quantities are as given below.

Data

For illustration, we shall use a sample employed in the Poisson example, in which $n = 10$, with scores as follows: 1.0, 2.0, 3.0, 4.0, 5.0, 6.0, 7.0, 8.0, 9.0, 10.0. (Of course, the data do not fit the normal model, but comparing the results obtained from use of the two models is of interest.)

Required Quantities

$n = 10$, and we set *mu* at 5.0. This leaves $\overline{x}$ and $s^2 = \hat{\sigma}^2$ to be calculated.

Steps in Calculation

1. Calculate

$$\overline{x} - \sum_{i=1}^{n} xi/n = \frac{1.0 + 2.0 + \cdots + 10.0}{10} = 5.5.$$

2. Calculate

$$\sum_{i=1}^{n} xi^2 = (1.0)^2 + (2.0)^2 + \cdots + (10.0)^2 = 385.0.$$

3. Calculate s^2. For this, a convenient formula is:

$$\frac{\sum_{i=1}^{n} xi^2 = n\overline{x}^2}{n} = \frac{385 - \frac{(10)(5.5)^2}{10}} = 8.25.$$

Note that we use N rather than $N-1$ in calculation s^2.

4.

$$s = \sqrt{s^2} = \sqrt{8.25} = 2.87.$$

5.

$$\frac{(\bar{x} - u)^2}{s} = \frac{(5.5 - 5.0)^2}{2.87} = .87108.$$

6. To get the quantity inside the square brackets in equation (A.3), we must add 1.0 to the result of step 5:

$$1.0 + .087108 = 1.087108.$$

7. This must be taken to the power $-(N/2) = -5$. This is the equivalent of findings:

$$(1.087108)^{-5} = .6586.$$

This is the *MRL* for the hypothesis $mu = 5.0$, where we use the term *mu* to indicate a hypothesized value of u. This compares with the value obtained by use of the Poisson distribution for the same hypothesis.

PROGRAM NORMAL LIKELIHOODS

This is a FORTRAN program to calculate the maximum relative likelihood for a mean from a normal population.

```
1   C
2   C
3   C      AGAIN WE RESERVE STORAGE SPACE.
4   C      SINCE WE ASSUME INTERVAL.
5   C      MEASUREMENT WE CREATE.
6   C      VARIABLES OF TYPE REAL.
7   C      DIMENSION X(100)
```

```fortran
8    C     REAL*4 MU
9    C     DATA SUM,DIV,XBAR,RMAX,ESP/5*0.0/
10   C
11   C     N= NO. OF CASES IN THE SAMPLE
12   C     MU= THE HYPOTHESIZED MEAN
           WHOSE RELATIVE LIKELIHOOD IS TO
           BE CALCULATED.
13   C     WE READ IN N, MU AND THE DATA
           WHICH IS IN ARRAY X(I).
14   C
15         READ(5,100) N,MU
16   100   FORMAT (15,F6.2)
17         DO 10 I=1,N
18         READ(5,101) X(1)
19   101   FORMAT (F6.2)
20   10    CONTINUE
21   C     NOW WE CAN CALCULATE SSQ, THE SUM OF SQUARES.
22         DO 15 1=1,N
23         SUM=SUM+X(1)
24         DIV=X(1)-MU
25         DIV=DIV*DIV
26         SSQ=SSQ+DIV
27   15    CONTINUE
28   C     NOW TO GET RL(MAX:U), USING THE
```

$$\text{FORMULA: } RL(\text{MAX:U}) = \left[1+\left(\frac{\bar{x}-mu}{\text{SQRT(VAR)}}\right)^{2}\right]^{\frac{N}{2}}$$

```fortran
29         XBAR=SUM/FLOAT (N)
```

```
30          VAR=SSQ/FLOAT (N-1)
31          VAR=SQRT (VAR)
32          RMAX=(XBAR-MU)/VAR
33          RMAX=1.0+RMAX**2
34          EXP=FLOAT (N)/2.0
35          RMAX=(1.0/RMAX)**EXP
36          WRITE(6.500) N,MU,(X(1) , 1=1,N)
37   C      CALCULATIONS COMPLETE:  WRITE OUT THE
38          DATA AND THE RESULTS.  WE CAN
39          RERUN THE PROGRAM ON SUCCESSIVE
40          BATCHES OF DATA.  TO GET JRLS
41          WE MUST MULTIPLY TOGETHER THE
42          RESULTS FROM EACH INDIVIDUAL RUN.
43   500    FORMAT(1H1/1X,'NO IN THE SAMPLE =' ,15/
44         *1X,'MEAN OF POPULATION =' ,F6,2/
45         *1X,'INPUT DATA'//(1X,10F6.2))
46          WRITE (6,501) XBAR,VAR,RMAX
47   501    FORMAT (///1X,,'MEAN OF SAMPLES
48         =' , F10.3//
49         *1X,'STANDARD DEVIATION =
50         'F10.3//
51         *1X,'MAXIMUM RELATIVE LIKELIHOOD
52         =',F10.3////)
53          STOP
54          END
```

NOTES

1. Lines 2 and 3 give the data for a 2×2 table, line 4 gives the baseline proportion, and lines 5 to 13 give nine hypothesized proportions, each of which is to be tested by the program. This is done by calculating RL's.

2. This translates into "run the FORTRAN program with 'source cards' (SCARDS) in the file named S.PLOT2." The program is compiled without errors being found, and the compiled program is placed in "$-$ LOAD," a temporary file. The command $R $-$ LOAD $ executes the compiled program, using data from the file LOAD, listed above. To follow the steps in the execution of the program, refer to the FORTRAN program given above.

3. P_{21} is the proportion in the control group closest to the baseline proportion of .49, $PHAT_{21}$ is the MLE for the control group, and $PHAT_{11}$ is the MLE for the experimental group.

4. The RB's are joint relative likelihoods. The ALPHA values are the corresponding values of the log of the average difference of the odds (see the program listing above).

5. In this example we have worked out 9 JRL's for hypothesized values of P_{11}, assuming a baseline value of .50 for P_{21}. This baseline value was determined from prior information, plus the observed sample value of P_{21}, which is equal to .55. On this assumption the most likely value of P_{11} is .50, with .40 a close second. Note also that the JRL for the P_{11} value of .30 is .29, essentially the same as the value of .286 obtained above.

6. This compiles the FORTRAN program in the file POISSON.

7. The compiled program is placed in the temporary file $-$ LOAD. This $R command instructs the computer to run the program using the data in the file DATA.

203

REFERENCES

Aaron, H. J. 1978. *Politics and the Professors: The Great Society in Perspective.* Washington, D.C.: Brookings Institution.

ADP (Area Development Project). *Research Monograph III.* 1969. Vancouver: United Community Services of Greater Vancouver.

Aigner, D. J. 1968. *Principles of Statistical Decision Making.* New York: Macmillan.

Anderson, M. 1980. "Welfare Reform." In *The United States in the 1980s.* Stanford, Calif.: Hoover Institution.

Anderson, S. B., and Ball, S. 1978. *The Profession and Practice of Program Evaluation.* San Francisco: Jossey-Bass.

Attkisson, C. C., and Others, eds. 1978. *Evaluation of Human Service Programs.* New York: Academic Press.

Barnett, V. 1973. *Comparative Statistical Inference.* New York: Wiley.

Barron, S. A. 1980. *Report of Pilot Project: Nerve Conduction Determinations at "Love Canal."* Buffalo Department of Neurology, School of Medicine, State University of New York at Buffalo.

Bennett, C. A., and Lumsdaine, A. A. 1975. *Evaluation and Experiment.* New York: Academic Press.

Bergin, A. E., and Strupp, H. H. 1972. *Changing Frontiers in the Science of Psychotherapy.* Chicago and New York: Aldine/Atherton.

Bethe, H. A. 1976. "The Necessity of Fission Power." 1976. *Scientific American* 234 (1):21–31.

Blalock, H. M., ed. 1974. *Measurement in the Social Sciences*. Chicago: Aldine.

Boruch, R. F., and Gomez, H. 1979. "Measuring Impact: Power Theory in Program Evaluation." In *Improving Evaluations*, edited by L. Datta and R. Perloff. Beverly Hills, Calif.: Sage.

Briar, S. 1963. "Clinical Judgment in Foster Care Placement." *Child Welfare* 42:161–69.

Bross, I. D. J. 1980. "Muddying the Water at Niagara." *New Scientist* 11:728–29.

Brown, G. E. 1968. *The Multiproblem Dilemma*. Metuchen, N.J.: Scarecrow Press.

Brown, M. 1979. "Setting Occupational Health Standards: The Vinyl Chloride Case." In *Controversy: The Politics of Technical Decisions*, edited by D. Nelkin. Beverly Hills, Calif.: Sage Publications.

Bupp, I. C. 1979. "The Nuclear Stalemate." In *Energy Futures*, edited by R. Stobaugh and D. Yergin. New York: Ballantine Books.

Bupp, I. C., and Derian, J. 1978. *Light Water*. New York: Basic Books.

Campbell, D. T. 1972. "Measuring the Effects of Social Innovations by Means of Time Series." In *Statistics: A Guide to the Unknown,* edited by J. M. Tanar et al. San Francisco: Holden-Day.

Campbell, D. T., and Stanley, J. C. 1963. *Experimental and Quasi-Experimental Designs for Research*. Chicago: Rand McNally.

Campbell, R. R. 1980. "Your Health and the Government." In Duignan and Rabushka (1980).

Cleary, A. T.; Linn, R.; and Walster, W. 1970. "Effect of Reliability and Validity on Power of Statistical Tests." In *Sociological Methodology*, edited by E. F. Borgatta and G. W. Bohrnstedt. San Francisco: Jossey-Bass.

Cohen, J. 1969. *Statistical Power Analysis for the Behavioral Sciences*. New York: Academic Press.

Cohen, P. C., and Krause, M. S. 1971. *Casework with Wives of Alcoholics*. New York: Family Service Association of America.

Coleman, J. S. 1964. *Models of Change and Response Uncertainty*. Englewood Cliffs, N.J.: Prentice-Hall.

———. 1974. *Power and the Structure of Society*. New York: Norton.

Coleman, J. S., and Others. 1966. *Equality of Educational Opportunity*. Washington, D.C.: U.S. Government Printing Office.

Collingridge, D. 1980. *The Social Control of Technology*. Milton Keynes, England: Open University Press.

Cook, T. J., and Campbell, D. T. 1976. "The Design and Conduct of Quasi-Experiments and True Experiments in Field Settings." In *Handbook of Industrial and Organizational Psychology*, edited by M. D. Dunnette. Chicago: Rand McNally.

Crane, J. A., 1974. *Employment of Social Service Graduates in Canada*. Ottawa: Canadian Association of Schools of Social Work.

———. 1976. "The Power of Social Intervention Experiments to Discriminate Differences between Experimental and Control Groups." *Social Service Review* 50 (2):224–42.

──────. 1980. "Relative Likelihood Analysis versus Significance Tests." *Evaluation Review* 4 (6):824–42.

Crane, J. A.; Poulos, S.; and Reimer, L. 1970. *An Experiment in the Deployment of Welfare Aides*. Vancouver: Research Department, Children's Aid Society of Vancouver.

Cronbach, L. J., and Associates. 1980. *Toward Reform of Program Evaluation*. San Francisco: Jossey-Bass.

Croxton, E. E., and Cowden, D. J. 1939. *Applied General Statistics*. Englewood Cliffs, N.J.: Prentice-Hall.

Donagan, A. 1977. *The Theory of Morality*. Chicago: University of Chicago Press.

Doub, W. O. 1974. "Meeting the Challenge to Nuclear Energy Head-On." *Atomic Energy Law Journal* 15 (6):261, 263.

Duignan, P., and Rabushka, A., eds. 1980. *The United States in the 1980s*. Stanford, Calif.: Hoover Institution.

Duncan, O. D. 1975. *Introduction to Structural Equation Models*. New York: Academic Press.

Eckler, B., and Segal & Company Ltd. 1976. *Report on Actuarial Aspects of Workers' Compensation Board of British Columbia*. Vancouver.

Edsall, J. T. 1981. "Two Aspects of Scientific Responsibility." *Science* 212 (4490): 11–14.

Edwards, A. W. F. 1972. *Likelihood*. Cambridge: Cambridge University Press.

Ekman, G. 1961. "A Simple Method for Fitting Psychophysical Power Functions." *Journal of Psychology* 51:343–50.

Fairweather, G. W., and Tornatzky, L. G. 1977. *Experimental Methods for Social Policy Research*. Oxford: Pergamon Press.

Filstead, W. J. 1981. "Using Qualitative Methods in Evaluation Research." *Evaluation Review* 5 (2):259–68.

Fischer, J. 1973. "Is Casework Effective? A Review." *Social Work* 18:5–21.

──────. 1976. *The Effectiveness of Social Casework*. Springfield, Ill.: Charles C. Thomas.

──────. 1978. *Effective Casework Practice: An Eclectic Approach*. New York: McGraw-Hill.

Fisher, R. A. 1973. *Statistical Methods and Scientific Inference*, 3rd ed. New York: Hafner Press.

Fraser, D. A. S. 1976. *Probability and Statistics: Theory and Applications*. No. Scituate, Mass.: Duxbury Press.

Freund, J. E. 1971. *Mathematical Statistics*, 2nd ed. Englewood Cliffs, N.J.: Prentice-Hall.

Fried, C. 1970. *An Anatomy of Values*. Cambridge, Mass.: Harvard University Press.

Galtung, J. 1977. *Methodology and Ideology*. Copenhagen: Christian Ejlers.

Geismar, L. L. 1969. *Preventive Intervention in Social Work*. Metuchen, N.J.: Scarecrow Press.

──────. 1971. *Family and Community Functioning*. Metuchen, N.J.: Scarecrow Press.

Geismar, L. L., and Ayres, B. 1960. *Measuring Family Functioning.* St. Paul, Minn.: Family Centered Project, Greater St. Paul Community Chest and Councils, Inc.

Gersuny, C. 1981. *Work Hazards and Industrial Conflict.* Hanover, N.H.: University Press of New England.

Gil, D. 1976. *The Challenge of Social Equality.* Cambridge, Mass.: Schenkman.

Glass, G. V. 1976. "Introduction." In *Evaluation Studies Review Annual,* vol. 1. Beverly Hills, Calif.: Sage.

Gold, D. 1969. "Statistical Tests and Substantive Significance." *American Sociologist* 4 (1):42–46.

Goodwin, L. 1979. "Limitations of the Seattle and Denver Income Maintenance Analysis." *American Journal of Sociology* 85 (3):653–57.

Gregg, G., and Associates. "The Caravan Rolls On: Forty Years of Social Problem Research." *Knowledge* 1 (1):31–61.

Gruber, M. L. 1980. "Inequality in the Social Services." *Social Service Review* 54 (1):59–75.

Hamblin, R. L. 1966. "Ratio Measurement and Sociological Theory: A Critical Analysis." Unpublished manuscript, Department of Sociology, Washington University, St. Louis, Mo.

————. 1974. "Social Attitudes: Magnitude Measurement and Theory." In *Measurement in the Social Sciences,* edited by H. M. Blalock, Jr. Chicago: Aldine.

Hamblin, R. L.; Buckholdt, D.; Ferritor, D.; Kosloff, M.; and Blackwell, L. 1971. *The Humanization Processes.* New York: Wiley.

Hannan, M. T.; Tuma, N. B.; and Groenveld, L. O. 1979. "Reply to Goodwin." *American Journal of Sociology* 85 (3):186–90.

Haynes, S. N., and Wilson, C. C. 1979. *Behavioral Assessment.* San Francisco: Jossey-Bass.

Holden, C. 1980. "Love Canal Residents under Stress." *Science* 208:1242–44.

House, E. R. 1980. *Evaluating with Validity.* Beverly Hills, Calif.: Sage.

Hudson, W., and Glisson, D. 1976. "Assessment of Marital Discord in Social Work Practice." *Social Service Review* 50 (2):293–311.

Ison, T. G. 1977. *Human Disability and Personal Income.* Queens University at Kingston, Ont.: Industrial Relations Centre.

Iverson, G. R. 1970. "Statistics according to Bayes." In *Sociological Methodology,* edited by E. F. Borgatta. San Francisco: Jossey-Bass.

Jenkins, S. 1974. "Child Welfare as a Class System," In *Children and Decent People,* edited by A. Schorr. New York: Basic Books.

Jöreskog, K. G., and Sörbom, D. 1979. *Advances in Factor Analysis and Structural Equation Models.* Cambridge, Mass.: Abt Books.

Kadushin, A. 1971. "Child Welfare." In *Research in the Social Services,* edited by Henry S. Maas. New York: National Association of Social Workers.

Kalbfleisch, J. G. 1975. *Probability and Statistical Inference,* rev. ed., vols. 1 and 2. Waterloo, Ont.: University of Waterloo.

Kaplan, A. 1964. *The Conduct of Enquiry.* San Francisco: Chandler.

Kogan, L. S., and Hunt, J. McV. 1950. *Measuring Results in Social Casework.* New York: Family Service Association of America.

Krantz, D. H. 1972. "A Theory of Magnitude Estimation and Cross-Modality Matching." *Journal of Mathematical Psychology* 9:168–99.

Levine, M. 1980. "Letter to the Editor." *Science* 211:8.

Lofland, J. 1971. *Analyzing Social Settings.* Belmont, Calif.: Wadsworth.

Lovins, A., and His Critics. 1977. *The Energy Controversy: Soft Path Questions and Answers.* San Francisco: Friends of the Earth.

Lowrance, W. D. 1976. *Of Acceptable Risk: Science and the Determination of Safety.* Los Altos, Calif.: Kaufmann.

Luce, R. D. 1972. "What Sort of Measurement Is Psychophysical Measurement?" *American Psychologist* 27:96–106.

Lyons, D. 1964. *Forms and Limits of Utilitarianism.* Oxford: Clarendon Press.

Maas, H. S., ed. 1971. *Research in the Social Services: A Five-Year Review.* New York: National Association of Social Workers.

MacIntyre, A. 1977. "Utilitarianism and Cost-Benefit Analysis: An Essay on the Relevance of Moral Philosophy to Bureaucratic Theory." In Sayre (1977).

Magidson, J. 1977. "Toward a Causal Model Approach for Adjusting for Preexisting Differences in the Nonequivalent Control Group Situation: A General Alternative to ANCOVA." *Evaluation Quarterly* 1:399–420.

Maher, E. 1977. "The Dynamics of Growth in the U.S. Electric Power Industry." In Sayre (1977).

Mallar, C. D., and Thornton, C. 1978. "Transitional Aid for Released Prisoners: Evidence from the Life Experiment." *Journal of Human Resources* 23 (2):208–36.

Manchester Guardian. 1981. "The Poison of the Playgrounds." April 14, editorial, p. 4.

Manne, A. S., and Richels, R. G. 1980. "Evaluating Nuclear Fuel Cycles." *Energy Policy* (March):3–16.

McCabe, A. 1967. *The Pursuit of Promise.* New York: Community Service Society of New York.

McCleary, R., and Hay, R. A., Jr. 1980. *Applied Time Series Analysis.* Beverly Hills, Calif.: Sage.

McGilly, F. 1978. "My Analysis, Your Ideology, His Bias." *Canadian Journal of Social Work Education* 4 (2, 3):94–108.

McGregor, W. 1968. "*A Q-Sort Study of Family Centered Casework Performance.*" M.S.W. thesis, University of British Columbia, Vancouver.

McKim, V. 1977. "Social and Environmental Values in Power Plant Licensing: A Study in the Regulation of Nuclear Power." In Sayre (1977).

Miller, G. H., and Willer, B. 1977. "Information Systems for Evaluation and Feedback in Mental Health Organizations." In *Evaluation Research Methods,* edited by L. Rutman, Beverly Hills, Calif.: Sage.

Moore, T. G. 1980. "Energy Options." In Duignan and Rabushka (1980).

Morrison, P. E., and Henkel, R. E., eds. 1970. *The Significance Test Contro-*

versy — A Reader. London: Butterworth.

Nagel, E. 1961. *The Structure of Science: Problems in the Logic of Scientific Explanation.* New York: Harcourt Brace Jovanovich.

Neave, D. 1970. *"Agency-Client Planning as a Factor in the Admission of Children to Foster Care."* Mimeographed, School of Social Work, University of British Columbia, Vancouver.

Neyman, J., and Pearson, E. S. 1933. "On the Problem of the Most Efficient Tests of Statistical Hypotheses." *Philosophical Transactions of the Royal Society* 221:289–337.

Northup, E. 1969. *"Factors Predictive of Length of Foster Care."* M.S.W. thesis, School of Social Work, University of British Columbia, Vancouver.

Novick, M. R., and Jackson, P. H. 1974. *Statistical Methods for Educational and Psychological Research.* New York: McGraw-Hill.

Nunally, J. C. 1967. *Psychometric Theory.* New York: McGraw-Hill.

Overton, A.; Tinker, K. H.; and Associates. 1957. *Casework Notebook.* St. Paul, Minn.: Family Centered Project.

Parlett, M., and Hamilton, D. 1976. "Evaluation as Illumination." In *Evaluation Studies Review Annual,* vol. 1, edited by G. V. Glass. Beverly Hills, Calif.: Sage.

Patton, M. Q. 1978. *Utilization-Focused Evaluation.* Beverly Hills, Calif.: Sage.

———. 1980. *Qualitative Evaluation Methods.* Beverly Hills, Calif.: Sage.

Phillips, B. S. 1976. *Social Research: Strategy and Tactics.* New York: Macmillan; London: Collier.

Phillips, L. D. 1972. *Bayesian Statistics for Social Scientists.* London: Nelson.

Picciano, D. 1980. *Pilot Cytogenic Study of the Residents of Love Canal, New York.* Houston: Biogenics Corporation.

Popper, K. R. 1965. *The Logic of Scientific Discovery.* New York: Harper & Row.

Rainwater, L. 1974. *What Money Can Buy: The Social Meaning of Poverty.* New York: Basic Books.

Rawls, J. 1972. *A Theory of Justice.* Cambridge, Mass.: Harvard University Press.

Reid, W. J., and Shyne, A. W. 1969. *Brief and Extended Casework.* New York: Columbia University Press.

Rein, M.; Nutt, T. E.; and Weiss, H. 1974. "Foster Family Care: Myth and Reality." In *Children and Decent People,* edited by Alvin Schorr. New York: Basic Books.

Ross, P. S., and Partners, Management Consultants. 1976. *Review of Organization and Administration.* Vancouver: Workers' Compensation Board of British Columbia.

Rossi, P., and Williams, W., eds. 1972. *Evaluating Social Programs; Theory, Practice, and Politics.* New York: Seminar Press.

Rossi, P., and Williams, W., eds. 1972. *Evaluating Social Programs: Theory Practice and Politics.* New York: Seminar Press.

Rotblat, J. 1981. "Hazards of Low-Level Radiation — Less Agreement, More Confusion." *Bulletin of the Atomic Scientists* 3 (6):31–36.

Rottenberg, S., ed. 1973. *The Economics of Crime and Punishment.* Washington, D.C.: American Enterprise Institute for Public Policy Research.

Rowe, W. D. 1976. *An Anatomy of Risk*. New York: Wiley.

Savage, I. R. 1968. *Statistics: Uncertainty and Behavior*. Boston: Houghton Mifflin.

Sayre, K., ed. 1977. *Values in the Electric Power Industry*. So. Bend, Ind.: University of Notre Dame Press.

Scioli, F. P., Jr., and Cook, T. J. 1975. *Methodologies for Analyzing Public Policies*. Lexington, Mass.: Lexington Books.

Shinn, A. M. 1969. *"The Application of Psychophysical Scaling Techniques to Measurement of Political Variables."* Mimeographed, Institute for Research in Social Science, University of North Carolina, Chapel Hill.

Shrader-Frechette, K. S. 1980. *Nuclear Power and Public Policy*. Dordrecht, The Netherlands: Reidel.

Shyne, A. 1973. "Research in Child-Caring Institutions." In *Child Caring: Social Policy and the Institution,* edited by D. M. Pappenfort, D. M. Kilpatrick, and R. W. Roberts. Chicago: Aldine.

Smith, R. J. 1980. "Love Canal Reviewed." *Science* 211:513.

Spiegel, M. R. 1961. *Statistics*. Schaum's Outline Series. New York: McGraw-Hill.

Stake, R. E. 1978. "The Case Study Method in Social Enquiry." *Educational Researcher* 7:5-8.

Stevens, S. S. 1956. "The Direct Estimation of Sensory Magnitudes: Loudness." *American Journal of Psychology* 69:1-25.

———. 1962. "The Surprising Simplicity of Sensory Metrics." *American Psychologist* 17:29-39.

———. 1966. "A Metric for the Social Consensus." *Science* 151:530-41.

Thomas, L., and Associates. 1980. *Report of the Governor's Panel to Review Scientific Studies and the Development of Public Policy on Problems Resulting from Hazardous Wastes*. Albany, N.Y.: Governor's Office.

Thompson, M. 1980. *Benefit-Cost Analysis for Program Evaluation*. Beverly Hills, Calif.: Sage.

Tripodi, T.; Fellin, P.; and Meyer, H. J. 1969. *The Assessment of Social Research*. Itasca, Ill.: F. E. Peacock.

Tuma, N. B., and Robins, P. 1980. "A Dynamic Model of Employment Behavior: An Application to the Seattle and Denver Income Maintenance Experiments." In *Evaluation Studies Review Annual*, vol. 5, edited by Ernst W. Stromsdorfer and George Farkus. Beverly Hills, Calif.: Sage.

U.S. Nuclear Regulatory Commission. 1975. *Reactor Safety Study — An Assessment of Accident Risks in U.S. Commercial Nuclear Power Plants*. Report No. WASH-1400. Washington, D.C.: U.S. Government Printing Office.

Vianna, N. J. 1980. "Adverse Pregnancy Outcomes in the Love Canal Area." Draft, New York State Department of Health, Albany.

Wallace, D. 1967. "The Chemung County Evaluation of Casework Services to Dependent Multi-Problem Families: Another Problem Outcome." *Social Service Review* 41 (4):379-89.

Walster, G. W., and Cleary, T. A. 1970. "Statistical Significance as a Decision Rule." In *Sociological Methodolgy,* edited by E. F. Borgatta and Others. San Francisco: Jossey-Bass.

Warren, R. 1968. "The Chemung County Experiment." In *The Multiproblem Dilemma*, edited by G. E. Brown. Metuchen, N.J.: Scarecrow Press.

Weiler, P. C. 1980. *Reshaping Workers' Compensation for Ontario: A Report Submitted to Robert G. Elgie, M.D., Minister of Labour*. Toronto: Workers' Compensation Board.

Whalen, R. P.; Herdman, R. C.; Haugrie, G. E.; Campbell, L. E.; Axelrod, D.; and Vianna, N. 1978. "Love Canal: Public Health Time Bomb." A Special Report to the Governor, Department of Health, State of New York, Albany.

Wilson, S. 1979. "Explorations of the Usefulness of Case Study Evaluations." *Evaluation Quarterly* 3 (3):446–59.

Zimbalist, S. 1977. *Historic Themes and Landmarks in Social Welfare Research*. New York: Harper & Row.

Zimring, F. E. 1975. "Firearms and Federal Law: The Gun Control Act of 1968." *Journal of Legal Studies* 4 (1):133–98.

NAME INDEX

Aaron, Henry J., 14, 24, 62
Aigner, Dennis J., 127, 129
Anderson, Marvin, 41
Anderson, S. B., 2, 25
Attkisson, C. C., 3, 11, 107
Ayres, B., 82, 98, 99, 100, 133, 140,
    150, 152, 153, 154

Ball, S., 2, 25
Barnett, V., 66, 132
Barron, Stephen A., 162
Bennett, Carl A., 8
Bergin, Allen E., 63
Bethe, H. A., 30, 47, 48
Blalock, H. M., 76
Boruch, Robert, 93, 154
Briar, Scott, 51
Bross, Irwin, 16, 39, 162, 163, 164,
    165, 166, 169

Brown, Gordon E., 151
Brown, Michael, 21, 43, 56
Bupp, Irvin C., 26, 46

Campbell, D. T., 10, 26, 58, 64
Campbell, Rita Ricardo, 41
Cleary, Anne T., 89, 90, 91, 154
Cohen, Jerome, 89, 94, 102, 141, 155,
    157, 165
Cohen, P. C., 159
Coleman, James, 5, 28, 39, 83
Collingridge, David, 3, 12, 21, 22, 62
Cook, Thomas J., 4, 11, 26
Cowden, D. J., 164
Crane John A., 16, 17, 69, 95, 115,
    124
Cronbach, Lee J., 2, 3, 11, 12, 15, 29,
    32, 33, 34, 58
Croxton, E. E., 164

Derian, Jean-Claude, 46
Donagan, Alan, 11
Doub, W. O., 13, 18
Duignan, Peter, 12
Duncan, Otis Dudley, 28

Eckler, Brown, 13
Edsall, John T., 23
Edwards, A. W. F., 5, 23, 115, 119
Ekman, G., 82

Fairweather, George W., 4
Fellin, P., 106
Filstead, William J., 36, 37
Fischer, Joel, 15, 83, 106
Fisher, R. A., 65
Fraser, D. A., 66
Freeman, Howard, 3, 4, 11, 15, 25, 26,
    27, 150
Freund, John, 93
Fried, Charles, 11

Galtung, Johan, 126
Geismar, Ludwig, 82, 98, 99, 100,
    133, 140, 150, 152, 153, 154
Gersuny, Carl, 39, 68
Gil, David, 50
Glass, Gene V., 2
Glisson, Dianne, 116, 117
Gold, D., 52
Gomez, Hernando, 93, 154
Goodwin, Leonard, 14
Gregg, Gary, 49
Gruber, Murray L., 39, 50, 51, 52

Hamblin, Robert L., 10, 67, 76, 77,
    79, 80, 82, 83, 84, 164
Hamilton, D., 37
Hannan, Michael T., 14
Hay, Richard A., 28
Haynes, Stephen N., 59
Henkel, R. E., 17, 66
Holden, Constance C., 163, 165
House, Ernest C., 28, 106, 107

Hudson, Walter, 116–17
Hunt, J. McV., 69, 116, 133

Ison, Terence G., 13
Iverson, G. R., 127, 129

Jackson, Paul A., 22, 127
Jenkins, Shirley, 50
Jöreskog, K. G., 4, 28

Kadushin, Alfred, 151
Kalbfleisch, J., 115, 155
Kaplan, Abraham, 14, 24, 57, 59
Kogan, L. S., 69, 116, 133
Krantz, D. H., 84
Krause, M. S., 159

Levine, Murray, 163
Lewin, Kurt, 11
Linn, R., 89, 90, 91, 154
Lofland, John, 36
Lovins, Amory, 46
Lowrance, W. D., 30
Luce, R. D., 76, 84
Lumsdaine, Arthur, 8
Lyons, David, 40

Maas, H. S., 152
MacIntyre, Alasdair, 48, 50
Magidson, J., 28
Maher, Ellen, 50
Mallar, C. D., 20, 61, 100
Manne, Alan S., 29
McCleary, Richard, 28
McGilly, Frank, 67
McGregor, W., 92, 93, 140
McKim, Vaughan, 50
Meyer, H. J., 106
Miller, Gary, 107
Moore, Thomas Gale, 42
Morrison, D. E., 17, 66

Nagel, E., 24, 57
Neave, Davis, 39, 50, 56

Neyman, J., 43
Northup, Everett, 56, 59
Novick, Melvin R., 22, 127
Nunally, J., 59, 94
Nutt, T. E., 50

Overton, Alice, 98

Parlett, M., 37
Patton, M. Q., 11, 32, 33, 35, 36, 37, 59, 107
Pearson, E. S., 43
Phillips, Bernard, 59
Phillips, Lawrence, 127, 140, 144
Picciano, D., 162
Popper, K. R., 23
Poulos, Susan, 69

Rabushka, Alvin, 12
Rainwater, Lee, 76, 81
Rasmussen, N., 30, 47, 48
Rawls, John, 11, 23, 35, 43, 44, 67, 68
Reid, William, 121
Reimer, Louis, 69
Rein, Martin, 50
Richels, Richard G., 29
Robins, Philip K., 10, 28
Ross, P. S., 13
Rossi, P., 3, 4, 11, 15, 25, 26, 27, 83, 150
Rotblat, Joseph, 10, 17, 20, 22, 24
Rottenberg, Simon, 19
Rowe, William D., 2, 12, 59

Savage, I. Richard, 129
Sayre, Kenneth, 46
Scioli, Frank, 11
Segal & Company, 13

Shinn, A. M., 76, 77, 82
Shrader-Frechette, K. S., 2, 3, 12, 18, 22, 30, 44, 46, 47, 48
Shyne, Anne, 51, 121
Smith, Jeffrey, 163
Sörbom, D., 4, 28
Spiegel, Murray R., 6, 26, 118, 165, 166
Stake, R. E., 11, 32, 36, 37, 38
Stanley, J. C., 10, 58
Stevens, S. S., 76, 77, 82
Strupp, Hans H., 63

Thomas, Lewis, 16, 162, 163
Thompson, Mark, 26
Thornton, Craig, 20, 61, 100
Tinker, K., 98
Tornatzky, Louis, 4
Tripodi, Tony, 106
Tuma, Nancy Brandon, 10, 28

Vianna, N. J., 162

Wallace, David, 151, 153
Walster, G. William, 89, 90, 91, 154
Warren, Roland, 155
Weiler, Paul, 3
Weiss, Heather, 50
Whalen, Robert P., 16, 161, 162, 164
Willer, Barry, 107
Williams, W., 83
Wilson, C. Chrisman, 59
Wilson, Steve, 36, 37, 38
Wright, Sonia R., 3, 4, 11, 15, 25, 26, 27, 39, 150

Zimbalist, Sidney, 156
Zimring, Franklin E., 57

SUBJECT INDEX

Adequacy, 1, 54
  of corrections measures, 56
Alternative hypotheses, 87–88
  specification of, 113–14
  and threshold effect, 87
Applied scientific research methods
    approach, 9, 10, 15
  and benefit/cost analysis, 26
  and evaluation questions, 25
  general critique of, 28–29
  methods in, 26
  and problem of naturalism, 30–32
  and scientist and citizen, 27–28
  and significant effects, 26
  and social inquiry, 24–25
  and uncertain inferences, 27
  and valuation, 25
  and values and data, 26

Area Development Project of Van-
    couver, 151, 156
  significance plot of findings in,
    157–59

Bayesian inference, 127–28
  used to reinterpret classical signifi-
    cance test, 131–36

Chemung County evaluation, 151, 156
  significance plot of findings in,
    157–59
Child welfare project, 97–98
Comprehensive evaluation, 61–64
  and policy formulation questions,
    61–62, 64
  and policy implementation questions,
    62–63, 64
  and policy outcome questions, 63–64

Data collection, 59–60
Decision rule, 132
  Bayesian, 134, 135–36
Democratic involvement, 54, 55, 64
Diachronic sampling, 126–27
Directed social change, 9, 32–39. *See
    also* Evaluation as education;
    Qualitative case study approach;
    Utilization-focused evaluation

Effectiveness of policies, 1, 54, 55
  of family counseling, 55
Egalitarian evaluation, 9, 11, 43–52
  critique of, 52
  critique of benefit/cost analysis in,
    48–49
  critique of nuclear power policy in,
    46–48
  critique of policies on institutional-
    ization in, 50–51
  and downward drift hypothesis,
    51–52
  and equity, 44
  and focus on corporate persons,
    49–50
  and inequality in the social services,
    50–52
  and interdisciplinary view of evalua-
    tion, 45
  and Rawls's principle, 44
  roles of citizen and scientist in, 46
  and significant effects, 45
  and social inquiry, 43
  and type 1 and type 2 errors, 45–46
  values in, 44
  values and observations in, 45
Equitableness, 1, 55
  of foster care admissions, 56
  of government regulation of toxic
    waste disposal, 56
  of occupational safety standards, 56
Errors, type 1 and 2, 4, 93–95, 100–05
  in egalitarian evaluation, 45–46
  in evaluation as applied scientific
    methods, 27

  in evaluation as scientific theory
    testing, 22
  in evaluative inference, 140–41, 142
  in TECH evaluation, 150, 157–60
  and use of raters, 100–05
  in utilitarian evaluation, 43
Evaluation, 1, 54. *See also* Applied
    scientific research methods ap-
    proach; Comprehensive evalua-
    tion; Egalitarian evaluation;
    Evaluation as education; Quali-
    tative case study approach;
    Scientific theory testing ap-
    proach; Utilitarian evaluation;
    Utilization-focused evaluation
  as applied scientific research, 1,
    19–32
  approaches to, 9
  as directed social change, 9, 32–38
  as a discipline, 2–3
  methods of, 4
  paradigms of, 9
  of policies controlling hazardous
    technologies, 2–3
  of policies governing instutionaliza-
    tion, 50–51
  of public policy on nuclear power,
    46–48
  of results of income maintenance
    experiments, 14
  of risk of birth abnormalities, 5
  roles of scientist and citizen in, 4,
    17–18, 23, 27, 37, 43, 46, 67–69
  roles of scientist and humanist in, 18
  scope of, 2, 54–57
  as social justice, 9, 65
  of social services, 2, 3, 5
  variables in, 2
Evaluation as education, 9, 10, 11,
    33–34
  classroom for, 34
  evaluator in, 34–35
  PSC in, 34
  uncertain inferences in, 35
  UTO and *UTO in, 35

valuation in, 35
Evaluation policies, 2
Evaluation and social justice, 40–52
Evaluative inference, 142–45
  overview of classification of methods
    of, 137–39

Implicit threshold hypotheses, 154–57
Inclusiveness of policies, 1, 54
Inferences, uncertain
  Bayesian, 5
  classification of methods in, 5
  conventionalism in, 65–66
  in evaluation as applied scientific
    research, 22–23, 27
  in evaluation as directed social
    change, 32–33, 37
  in evaluation as social justice, 45
  and likelihood, 5
  and naturalistic fallacy, 66
  nonprobabilistic, 5
  policy issues in, 4, 16–17, 65–67
  prior information in, 5
  role of values in, 66
  and significance test, 65
  and single-school versus eclectic ap-
    proaches, 66–67
Intervention effects, 90–91, 92–93
  inconsistent, 91–92
Invalidity, 91, 153

Joint relative likelihood, 121–22
  in evaluative inference, 141–42
  of hypotheses regarding rates of mis-
    carriage, 167–68

Local probability systems, 126–27
Likelihood, 119. *See also* Likelihood
  inference; Maximum likelihood;
  Maximum relative likelihood;
  Relative likelihood analysis
Likelihood functions, 118–19. *See also*
  Likelihood; Likelihood in-
  ference; Maximum likelihood;
  Maximum relative likelihood;

Relative likelihood analysis
Likelihood inference, 115
Logical flaws in Bethe and Rasmussen
  reports, 47–48
Loss function, 134
Love Canal research, 161–69
  described, 161–63
  index of effects in, 164
  reanalysis of data of, 164–66
  and reproductive abnormalities prob-
    lem, 162–69
  and science and social policy issues,
    169
  scientific controversies over, 161–63
  and seriousness of hazard, 169
  and type 1 and type 2 error prob-
    lems, 165–66

Magnitude estimation. *See* Value
  scaling
Maximum likelihood, 115–17
Maximum relative likelihood, 122–23
Measurement design in child welfare
  project, 98–99

Naturalistic fallacy, 30
  in significance tests, 30–31
Null hypothesis, 87–88, 89
  in TECH evaluation, 150

Outcome probability, 86–87, 89–90
  direct determinants of, 89–90
  and discrepancy measure, 88–89

Parameters, 125
  fixed, 138, 143–44
  fluctuating, 5, 125–26, 138, 142, 144
Patterning observations, 58, 59, 100
Plausibility, 113–15
  of hypotheses or possible findings,
    5, 17
  measurement of, 5, 114–15
  standard of, 114
Policy, 1
  approaches to evaluation of, 9

areas of, 2–3
definition of, 1
evaluation of, defined, 1
formulation of, 1
implementation of, 1
outcomes of, 2
to guide uncertain inferences, 4
Posterior distribution, 131
Power functions, 81–82
Prior distribution, 129–31, 139, 142,
    143, 144

Qualitative case study approach, 9, 11,
    35–38
claimed advantages of, 35
roles of scientist and citizen in, 37
uncertain inferences in, 37
valuation in, 36
values in (completeness; holism;
    particularism; value neutrality
    and pluralism), 36–37

Relative likelihood analysis, 119–21.
    See also Joint relative likelihood
in inference, 145
of Love Canal data, 167–69
and relative support in evaluative in-
    ference, 141
Relative origin. See Value scaling
Research design, 97–109
variations in, 105–07
Roles of scientist and citizen in evalua-
    tion. See Evaluation

Sample sizes, 90
Sample standard deviations, 90
Scientific theory testing approach, 9,
    10, 19–23
economic theory in, 19–20
limitations of, 23–24, 28–29
problem of naturalism in, 29–31
roles of scientists and lay persons in,
    23
rules of procedural validity in, 23
uncertain inferences in, 22–23

valuation in, 21
values in, 21
values and observations in, 21–22
Social worker performance, 92–93

TECH evaluation, 149–60
inference procedures in, 155–56
planned and unplanned features in,
    152–54
social work examples of, 151–52
Technical skew, 149–60
and TECH, 149–50
Threshold hypothesis, 73, 81, 100. See
    also Implicit threshold hypo-
    theses
and calibration of value scale,
    113–14

Unreliability, 90, 103–04, 153–54
Utilitarian evaluation, 9, 10, 12, 40–43
and constructs of utilitarianism, 40
and evaluation and social inquiry,
    40–41
and principle of utility, 40
and role of values in evaluation, 42
and roles of scientist and citizen, 43
and view of significant effects, 42–43
type 1 and type 2 errors in, 43
Utilization-focused evaluation, 9, 11
    32–33
roles of scientist and citizen in, 33
and valuation, 32
and values and observations, 33
and uncertain inferences, 33

Valuation, 9–69
and admissible and inadmissible
    values, 12–14
in applied scientific methods ap-
    proach, 25–26
of benefits of social services, 69
contexts of, 14
disputes over
    in assessing outcomes, 15
    in income maintenance, 14

in policy on nuclear power, 12
in public health, 16
in social work, 15
in workers' compensation, 13
in egalitarian evaluation, 44–45
in evaluation as education, 33
issues in, 12–16, 53–54
and observations, 4, 21–22, 26, 32,
    42, 44, 58–60, 73–109
problem of defining significance in,
    15
procedural fairness in, 67–68
process of, 15–17
in qualitative case study approach,
    35
of risks, 68
scientific approach to, 21
in scientific theory testing approach,
    21
selection of judges for, 68–69
specification of values as part of, in
    child welfare study, 97

in TECH evaluation, 150
in utilitarian evaluation, 43–44
in utilization-focused evaluation, 32
Value scaling, 4
alternative methods of, 74–75
bipolar, 82
dichotomous, and inference method,
    140, 142
and hypotheses, 5
and inference methods, 4–5
interval, 75
magnitude estimation in, 76–80,
    83–85, 99
ordinal, 75
power functions in, 81–82
ratio, 4, 75–76
relative origins in, 80–81
and research design, 4–5
technique of, 73
and threshold effects, 74
and units of value scale, 83
and use of multiple measures, 82